I0150429

ENCYCLOPEDIA OF

# HAUNTED NORTHERN INDIANA

## BY
## NICOLE KOBROWSKI

Unseenpress.com, Inc. PO Box 687 Westfield, IN 46074

For information contact:
Unseenpress.com, Inc.
PO Box 687
Westfield, IN 46074

Library of Congress Cataloging-in-Publication Data

Kobrowski, Nicole
    Unseenpress.com's Definitive Encyclopedia of Haunted Indiana/Nicole Kobrowski
            Includes index
  1. Ghosts Indiana;  2. Paranormal Indiana; 3. Indiana History; 4. Indiana Travel

Library of Congress Control Number: 2017900822
ISBN-13: 978-0-9986207-1-8


Printed in the United States of America

Published by
Haunted Backroads Books
an imprint of Unseenpress.com, Inc.
PO Box 687
Westfield, IN 46074

Although the authors and publisher have made every effort to ensure the accuracy and completeness of information contained in this book, we assume no responsibility for errors, inaccuracies, omissions or any inconsistency herein. Any slights of people, places or organizations are unintentional.

The Unseenpress.com, Inc. website is
http://www.unseenpress.com/

Cover design Unseenpress.com, Inc.

# Notes

# TABLE OF CONTENTS

# OTHER TITLES BY NICOLE KOBROWSKI

## Published by Unseenpress.com, Inc.
*(print and ebook)*

- Haunted Backroads: Central Indiana
- Haunted Backroads: Ghosts of Westfield
- Haunted Backroads: Ghosts of Madison County, Indiana
- Fractured Intentions: A History of Central State Hospital for the Insane
- She Sleeps Well: The Extraordinary Life and Murder of Dr. Helene Elise Hermine Knabe
- Unseenpress.com's Official Encyclopedia of Haunted Indiana
- Unseenpress.com's Official Encyclopedia of Haunted Northern Indiana
- Unseenpress.com's Official Encyclopedia of Haunted Central Indiana
- Unseenpress.com's Official Encyclopedia of Haunted Southern Indiana

## Published by IUPUI
Distance Learning: A Guide to System Planning and Implementation

(by Merrill, Young, and Kobrowski)


Published by Bildungsverlag EINS
Metal Line (Instructor's guide and workbook)
Hotel Line (Instructor's Guide)
Englisch für Elektroberufe (Instructor's guide and workbook)
Supply Line (Instructor's guide and workbook)
Construction Line (Instructor's guide and workbook)

## Coming soon!
Haunted Backroads: Ghosts of Hamilton County, Indiana
Audio books

# DEDICATION

*To hot tea and popcorn.*
*Two of my best friends.*

# About the Author

Nicole Kobrowski is the co-owner of Unseenpress.com, Inc., which was founded in 2001. She and her husband Michael started the business because of their interest in the paranormal and their love of history. She has written professionally under a variety of pen names for over 20 years, including books for ESL and dozens of articles on a myriad topics. Being a paranormal enthusiast for over 30 years, she has done investigation work in many areas including spirit photography, electronic voice phenomenon, and automatic writing. In addition to her work in the paranormal field, Nicole is an Adult Education Consultant. Currently, she lives in her "über haunted home" with her husband and Lyla, their rescued cat.

Unseenpress.com, Inc. is a paranormal book publisher and ghost tour operator. The company can be found on Facebook, Instagram and Twitter.

# PREFACE

Every book I write is a creative pleasure. With this particular book, I need to learn to cut the cord. Every time I was about to finish and send it off, someone (sometimes me) would let me know about another fascinating place that I think just has to be included.

When I originally wrote the book, I had been to about 33% of these locations. As of this writing, I have been to over 70%. By the next writing, I will have completed my goal of visiting every site listed.

As always, the intent of this book is to educate and to serve as a guide for paranormal enthusiasts, investigators and anyone traveling around the wonderful state of Indiana.

Special thanks to Emily Dickos-Carter and to Megan Norris.

I hope you enjoy it as much as I enjoyed writing it.

Nicole Kobrowski
January 2017

We love hearing from paranormal enthusiasts and investigators about their experiences at these locations or from other "haunted' locations. Send all enquiries or story submissions for future publications to customerservice@ unseenpress.com.

# A GUIDE TO THE ENCYCLOPEDIA

This book is set up in order for you to find information quickly and easily. The book is set up by counties, which you'll find at the top of each page. For each entry, I've developed a legend for your use as follows:

## Sample Entry

### Ceylon Covered Bridge

The name of the location.

**Geneva:** Two miles NE of Geneva on CR W950S just east of US 27.

The directions, address and supporting information.

This bridge originally crossed the Wabash River. Since the river shifted, the bridge now spans a back channel. It is considered the last standing covered bridge over any part of the Wabash River. Built by the Smith Brothers Company, it is a Howe Truss structure. At 126 feet long (140 feet including the seven feet overhang at each end), the bridge is now surrounded by a roadside park and is on the National Register of Historic Places.

The section entry contains background on events around the history and haunting.

A group of teenagers performing a séance saw a man as tall as the bridge itself. The man left a blood stain on the pentagram they were using on the floor of the structure. Some people believe this pentagram was a portal and today strange occurrences still take place.

# DO–IT–YOURSELF INVESTIGATIONS

Since starting Unseenpress.com, Inc. we've been approached by people and organizations on a weekly basis asking us if we'd investigate their home or asking if they can go with us to a "ghost hunt" or an "investigation". These aren't even including the places we approach for investigations. Unfortunately, we can't accommodate all requests- days only have 24 hours. As a result, we've referred some people to reputable paranormal groups so they connect with investigators in their area and we've worked with clients to find them reputable help in their area. Also, we have taken some experienced investigators on our investigations and had great success with it. We have also started education classes for people who want to take responsibility for their own hauntings. We'll talk more about that later.

Still, we find a fundamental difference in some of the requests- "ghost hunt" and "investigation". Both terms have very different meanings. Certain people want to go to haunted locations, be scared, talk about what they've experienced, make a quick determination it is haunted (or not) and move on to the next location. Other people want to conduct investigations that are scientifically documented, following set procedures.

## Before you go

Your team should have a clear idea of who they are and how they should behave before they ever set foot on the client's property. Standards should be explained and reviewed before the investigation.

Before you decide to go, we recommend the following standards:

- Get permission (See Permission section).
- Walk the area before the investigation. If you're doing a daytime investigation, this is not so important. If you're doing a night time investigation, you should do this step to understand where you might encounter difficulty. You should always do a walk through to understand the temperature fluctuations and EMF readings (however, how will you really know what a baseline is? You could be experiencing paranormal activity on your first visit).
- Meet at the location and decide who will do what and with what equipment.
- Offer a blessing, protection, or prayer if you wish.
- Walk around to decide where to place equipment.
- Take pictures, videos and audio recordings. Make notes about any changes in temperature, feelings you had or sightings. If everyone on your team does this, you should have an accurate picture of the investigation when you're finished. It helps eliminate non-paranormal causes for suspected activity.

Once you've made the necessary arrangements, consider the following points during an investigation.

- Never roam alone in an unfamiliar setting. You need to be safe.
- Take ID with you. You might need to prove who you are.
- Take a cell phone with you and let others know where you are going.
- If you will be in the field for a long time, take adequate food and drink with you. Eat only in specific areas to minimize noise and contamination of evidence.

- If you are asked to leave, do so without making a fuss. It will benefit you in the long run. Respect everyone living and dead.
- Don't smoke. It can contaminate photographic/video evidence.
- Use care when taking photos. Don't take photos when others are taking them. Note anything that could create false orbs in photos. Keep hair, fingers and camera straps away from the lens. You, equipment, or other items can cast false positive shadows so be aware of your location and equipment placement.
- Do not move audio recorders when speaking. It can create distortion.
- No drugs or alcohol before, during or after an investigation. If you're sick, stay home. Illegal drugs are a no. Drunk people on an investigation or after an investigation while still a part of the team is stupid and not good for the paranormal field or its image.
- Record any conditions that could affect data (humidity, dust, etc.).
- No noisy clothing, jewelry, keys, or change- these items affect what we hear.
- Apply no items that affect smell- cologne, perfume, etc. Do use fragrance-free deodorant.
- Dress for the field. Use your team's uniform or wear clean, weather appropriate clothes.
- Ensure hair is away from face- ponytails are good. Buns are even better.
- If you are frightened in a location- leave. Some of the most haunted places are in the middle of nowhere and you might have a bad encounter with a human. Use common sense.
- Have an emergency plan and make sure someone is on the team that is able to perform CPR and/or call for help quickly.

# Paranormal Investigation

## The Field
Much information is written about paranormal investigation. Some of it is stated in absolute terms. Paranormal investigation is a wide open field. I say field, because that is what it should be, however, to my knowledge, no one makes a living solely by investigating the paranormal- myself included. Certainly, research labs exist for parapsychology, which is completely different than paranormal investigation. Most investigators belong to organizations that support paranormal research, though, most everyone has a day job.

## Education Options
Along these same lines, there are no accredited degrees in paranormal investigation. None. Zero. Nada. Niet, Kein. Don't even waste your time and money. Many paranormal organizations offer certificate courses to become "certified" in paranormal investigation. Many paranormal groups charge dues and ask you to take classes (sometimes paying extra) in order to be "qualified" to go on investigations. As a lifelong student of Adult Education, I can hardly argue about basic training needed to safely go on an investigation. However, each organization has its own policies and procedures for accomplishing an investigation. You have to decide if they are sound, if you agree with them and if you'd like to be a part of the organization.

Knowing the state of education in the paranormal field, this difference begs the question, "what does being a certified paranormal investigator (or obtaining a certificate) get me? Some people believe it doesn't really benefit you. As it isn't a recognized field of work or science (yes, we are considered pseudo-scientists), it isn't going to raise your pay (unless you latch onto the media). Some people would argue the benefit comes in being certified to investigate with the organization that certified you. Other people argue that being certified or recognized by a certain group is motivation enough. They believe that this certification might get them into more places or give them more of an advantage. Again, it is up to your interpretation.

## *Media, Myths and Absolutes*

No one, no matter what experiences someone has had with the paranormal, knows what to expect or what concrete facts can be said about spirit activity. No one can concretely define what a ghost really is or if they exist. While I have definitions of some of the elements surrounding the paranormal and investigation, my take may be different than another investigator's definition. Also, I have most definite feelings about ghosts; I am a firm believer in them. Some people are out to disprove the existence of spirits.

The media also has its own take on the paranormal ranging from the cheesy "ghostbusters" type attitude to making it somewhat darker and more dramatic than what it really is. For example, shows exist for ratings. If television shows didn't have something scary and exciting, no one would watch them. Be careful what you consume.

Also, be careful about what you read and absorb. For example, an investigator on a popular television series said "A human spirit can only lift three to ten pounds." Really? How do we know this? Did this investigator have an interview with a ghost? Because if he did, I would love the transcript. Does this mean that when Arnold Schwarzenegger dies he is limited to lifting three to ten pounds? Or does he get to lift more because he was a body builder? Likewise another misconception is that the "haunting hours" are between 12-3am. If that were true, why do we have so many daytime reports of activity?

Absolute statements like the ones above are patently false until proven otherwise. If someone says conclusively, "Yep, you've got ghosts.", it is their own flavor and opinion- kind of like a certification that your house is haunted. Other investigators may disagree with the findings. While some people believe that ghosts can go home with you (as I do), there are other investigators who do not believe this.

## If we can't prove anything what is the point?

All we can do is conduct inquiry based on common assumptions and draw our own conclusions. However, surrounding investigative inquiry is more than just our opinions and biases. We also must take scientific method into account. In scientific inquiry, we decide what we're going to study, decide on an explanation for what we're studying, define how we'll research it, muse on the types of results you think you'll get, execute and analyze the plan. Scientific method is scientific method, no matter what area you are in. I am a scholar in Adult Education and I apply scientific method the same as anyone who has learned it. The focus of my research in Adult Education is different than that of a Sociologist.

You might ask what the problem is, that scientific inquiry seems very straightforward. It is, but what is contained in each step is the difference between mainstream, accepted science and the assumed pseudo-science of the paranormal. We can't test against what we don't know. Our tools have only been test driven to a certain point. For example, many investigators believe EMF detectors can indicate spirit activity. How do we know they aren't picking up power inside the walls, under the floor, etc.? There is a scale for what is normal for certain types of electromagnetic fields, but have we been able to consistently replicate what we're seeing as "abnormal" to be able to say it is truly abnormal and paranormal?

## Organizations and Investigations

Investigators employ several steps involved in paranormal investigation. Investigations aren't always exciting and many of them are hurry up and wait situations. Sometimes you get a hit and sometimes after hours of sitting or hours of analyzing, you get nothing. It can be frustrating, but also rewarding. The difference among investigators is how they conduct themselves, their groups and their investigations.

One bad experience can lead to a complete distaste for the paranormal in general. Two recent cases come to mind. First, the producers of a show about ghost children did an unauthorized ghost hunt and filming in Crown Hill Cemetery in Indianapolis, Indiana. While I believe there is much paranormal activity afoot in the cemetery, the cemetery staff made it quite clear that it wants nothing to do with the paranormal. The makers of the program misrepresented the history of the subject and also the history of Crown Hill. Additionally, they didn't ask permission to film on the grounds. They seemed to assume that because it was a cemetery, owned by the State (not true), it was fair game (also not true).

Another example is Central State Hospital also in Indianapolis. A "documentary" was produced on the premise that it would be historic in nature. It was historic all right, but not the historic documentary that was presented in the proposal to the city. Would you want to be affiliated with an organization that misrepresents itself?

## Reputation

Moving to the practical, keep in mind that the reputation of your organizations, investigations, and personal behavior is under scrutiny from the minute you approach an organization or individual about conducting an investigation. How you conduct your organization, investigations and/or personal behavior determine how much credibility each element has and how the paranormal community is perceived as a whole. For example, a group of investigators trespassed on a site where a well known serial killer lived. They took pictures and video and posted both on their website and a video sharing site. They even boasted about it on television. When the owner saw this evidence, the police became involved. What do you think about this group's ethics or credibility? I certainly wouldn't want to work with this group. Another group trespassed at Central State Hospital, several times. They were told by the police to stay away from the site but didn't. Now, they have a bad reputation with the police and have given paranormal investigation a bad name. Would you want these people coming into your home or business?

## Permission

Investigation doesn't mean glory. Too many times have I seen investigators jockey for position while investigating hauntings. With the exception of private homes, businesses, etc. any already known location has been investigated or hunted to some extent many time over. There is no "scooping" going on. For example, Central State Hospital in Indianapolis is the perceived as the Holy Grail of haunted locations. Who hasn't been out there? Most folks who have been here are employees, with the police or have done so illegally. What does claiming "first rights" do? Absolutely nothing. What does the trespassing do to the credibility of you, your organization and to the field? *Trespassing kills credibility.*

Many people say, "well how do you get in there?" or "I don't know how to get permission." Well, here's your guide. Find the owner and get permission. *Always get it in writing.*

## *Find the Owner*
*Property, including businesses, historic properties, "abandoned" properties, farms, woods, etc.*

Go to the township or county recorder and ask for the name of the owner on record for the property. This is public information that they have to give you. You can usually get a phone number as well. Contact the owners and if they don't respond, follow up. If they still don't respond or you get a resounding, "No," let it go. Remember, what you do and how you act reflects on not just you and your organization, but on everyone. Think about how you can revisit it at a future time and maybe change the no to a yes.

## Cemeteries
Go to the township trustee, who usually controls them. If your county has a cemetery commission, speak with them. If it is a large cemetery like Crown Hill that is run by an organization, talk to them. If it is a cemetery attached to a church, talk to the pastor, minister, priest, etc. Don't assume that because it is a cemetery that you can visit it any time you wish. Most cemeteries in Indiana close at dusk. Simply calling the police to let them know you're out there doesn't cover you. It is still under the control of others.

## Roads and Highways
For your own safety, if nothing else, you must have permission to create an obstruction or to be on these roads. If you are walking on the road, you run the risk of getting yourself killed. If you're with several people, you increase your risk. Many of the haunted roads are in areas where people live.

Once an organized ghost hunting group decided to trespass on a fairly well known area in Hamilton County. They even posted pictures on the internet showing them trespassing. The police were alerted by the owner and they received a notice telling them to take down all photos, videos, etc and that next time they would be prosecuted. How would you like to ask the boss at your day job for bail money?

# COUNTY MAP

The map on the following page shows a numbered county map. On the next page, these numbers correspond with the correct county.

Use the names as a quick reference to find the correct county in the book.

# County Map of Indiana

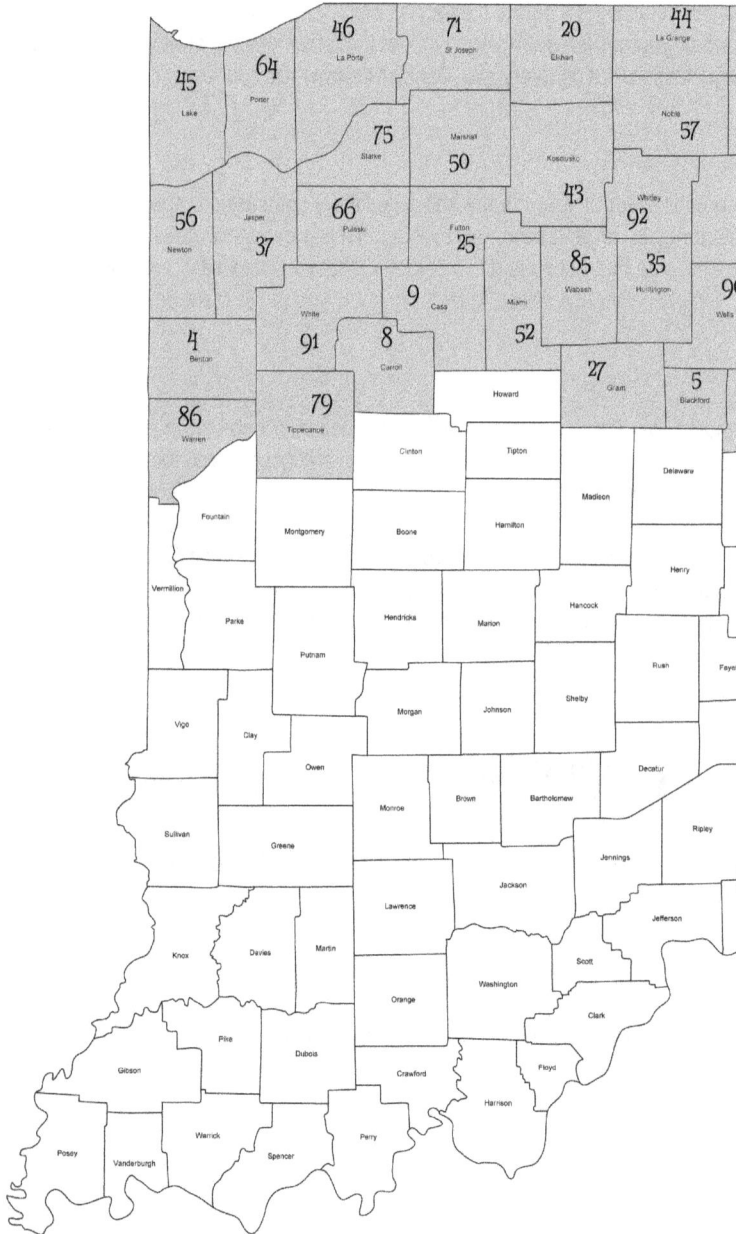

# ALPHABETICAL LIST OF INDIANA COUNTIES

| Number | Name | Number | Name |
|---|---|---|---|
| 1 | Adams | 71 | St. Joseph |
| 2 | Allen | 75 | Starke |
| 4 | Benton | 76 | Steuben |
| 5 | Blackford | 79 | Tippecanoe |
| 8 | Carroll | 85 | Wabash |
| 9 | Cass | 86 | Warren |
| 17 | DeKalb | 90 | Wells |
| 20 | Elkhart | 91 | White |
| 25 | Fulton | 92 | Whitley |
| 27 | Grant | | |
| 35 | Huntington | | |
| 37 | Jasper | | |
| 38 | Jay | | |
| 43 | Kosciusko | | |
| 44 | LaGrange | | |
| 45 | Lake | | |
| 46 | LaPorte | | |
| 50 | Marshall | | |
| 52 | Miami | | |
| 56 | Newton | | |
| 57 | Noble | | |
| 64 | Porter | | |
| 66 | Pulaski | | |

# ADAMS
# COUNTY

## Adams County Cheese Factory

*(reported razed)*
**Decatur:** In the woods east of the Kukelhan Mansion

*(See Kukelhan Mansion entry, Geneva, Adams County)*

This site was abandoned for many years then torn down. Active spirits are caretakers for the property. Some people describe experiencing feelings of uneasiness while other visitors feel a sense of peace.

## Ceylon Covered Bridge

**Geneva:** Two miles NE of Geneva on CR W950S just east of US 27.

This bridge originally crossed the Wabash River. Since the river shifted, the bridge now spans a back channel. It is considered the last standing covered bridge over any part of the Wabash River. Built by the Smith Brothers Company, it is a Howe Truss structure. At 126 feet long (140 feet including the seven feet overhang at each end), the bridge is now surrounded by a roadside park and is on the National Register of Historic Places.

A group of teenagers performing a séance saw a man as tall as the bridge itself. The man left a blood stain on the pentagram they were using on the floor of the structure. Some people believe this pentagram was a portal and today strange occurrences still take place.

## Kukelhan Mansion

**Geneva:** Just north of Decatur, east of US 27, not far from North Pointe sub-division

The house was owned by a wealthy banker who lost his mind. He was paranoid that people were after his money. Due to his illness, he killed his family and hung himself. Investigators report they are unable to be on the property for long periods of time because of uneasy feelings and the residual haunting replaying the hanging death.

## South Adams Middle School

**Geneva:** 105 W. Line St.

Staff including cooks, janitors, teachers and administration report a full apparition seen in the rafters when arriving at the building early in the morning and during evening events.

## Williams Covered Bridge
**Williams:** Huron and Williams Roads between SR450 and Port-Williams Rd.

Before the bridge was covered, a man went across on horseback and the horse jumped off. Also, an African-American man is said to have been hung on the bridge, ripping his head from his body.

Today, visitors see the rope swinging and hear screams. At either end of the bridge, a translucent apparition of a man is seen. You can hear horse hooves and the neighing of the animal. A phantom shadow figure also appears.

# ALLEN
# COUNTY

## 1530 North Harrison Street
**Fort Wayne:** 1530 N. Harrison St.

Former tenants report being physically touched by spirits that left marks. Growling noises and brown goo are reported. A demon rag doll reappears although it was burned.

## Blue Cast Magnetic Springs Sanitarium
**Woodburn:** Blue Cast Rd.

Visitors see shadows and red and blue orbs. Investigators report cold spots, footsteps and voices.

## Bostick Bridge
*(aka Turner Bridge)*
**Fort Wayne:** On Bostick Rd. between US 24 and US 27 just south of I-469.

This historic bridge is a Whipple truss (double intersection Pratt truss) bridge built in 1894 by the Canton Bridge Company. It spans 169 feet. Many people believe satanic activity performed here opened a portal to Hell. Investigators report hearing growling, seeing menacing red and white glowing eyes, and hearing the tortured cries of those unfortunates in Hell.

Luckily for you, now you can safely test out these theories. This bridge was rehabilitated into a pedestrian bridge and a new one was put in its place. The historic bridge was painstakingly restored with vintage techniques such as reproduced panels and in-kind hot metal riveting. In acquiescence to modern life, modern railing was added.

## Bruick Road
**New Haven:** Bruick Rd. runs N/S between SR 37 and US 24

A white light appears, grows in size and even changes colors. If you follow, it seems to move farther away from you and disappears.

## City Hall
**New Haven:** 428 Broadway St.
*(aka Historic City Hall)*

This building was built in 1913 and served as the courthouse, jail, fire station and a recruitment center during WWII. Investigators captured orbs and smells ranging from sulphur and sewer to cigars and perfume. Additionally, one visitor was chased out of the upstairs by rapid pounding on the wall around her. As she ran down the stairs, it followed her all the way out the front doors. When she exited, the doors closed behind her and she could still hear the pounding from the street. According to her, it went on for over five more minutes until it silenced. Some people believe these were the souls of the dead who were supposedly taken care of here when the building was used as a temporary morgue.

## Carroll High School
**Fort Wayne:** 3701 Carroll Rd.

Old stories state one junior at the school dies every year and comes back to haunt the building. A boy took the seat of one of these unfortunates and was rudely pushed off the seat.

## Cedar Canyons
*(aka Griffin Rd.)*
**Fort Wayne:** Griffin and Auburn Rds.

An old transparent man walks on this road near Cedar Canyons. The best time to see him is between 9:00pm and 5:00am.

## Chapman Road
**Fort Wayne:** North of Cedar Canyons Rd. to Chapman Rd. Turn right on Griffin Rd. and stop at the bottom of the hill.

Cars seem to be pulled up the road when they are put in park or neutral.

## Char's House of Oak
**Fort Wayne:** Was located on Wells St.
*Out of business*

This store used to sell oak furniture. There are reports of a man with messy black hair, an unshaven face, soiled undershirt and green workman's pants appears on the main staircase. He seems to be angry and takes his belt off, raising it to swing. People report a chilling cold and unsettled feeling when he passes through them.

## Cold Water Road Wal-Mart
**Fort Wayne:** 5311 Coldwater Road.

Between 3:00am-4:00am, bagpipes play. A man in a plaid kilt paces the floors. When he passes by you, a cold feeling settles on you. Although he hasn't interacted directly with staff or shoppers, he is friendly. Additionally, when he makes his appearance, items fall off shelves.

## Crossroads Cemetery
**Fort Wayne:** East side of Bethal Rd., south of Dupont Rd.

Visitors report moving lights, mysterious noises, feelings of being watched when in cemetery.

## Devil's Dip
**Georgetown:** Unknown

Local legend states the house at the bottom of this hill was home to a little girl who was hit by a car. If you drive too fast, the girl appears next to the telephone pole across from the house or she is also said to get into your back seat, cry, and tell you to slow down.

## Devil's Hollow
**Fort Wayne:** Two versions of the legend exist for this location. One is on Cedar Canyon Rd. between Canyon Run and Auburn Rd. The other is on Devil's Hollow Rd.

Orbs and faces have been caught on camera between 9 p.m. and 5 a.m. An old transparent man walks on this road near Cedar Canyons. ## Eel River Cemetery

**Dunn Mill:** Corner of Madden and Carroll Rds.

A tall, thin man in tan pants and a long coat walks the cemetery. When approached, he disappears. Sometimes he wears a dark hat and other times he smokes a cigarette. Investigators report the smell of smoke when he appears.

## Embassy Theater
**Fort Wayne:** 125 W. Jefferson Blvd.

This glorious theater opened on May 4, 1928 as the Emboyd Theater. Top-notch in every way, it boasted a pipe organ, vaudeville shows and the nearby Indiana Hotel. In 1952, the theater was sold to the Alliance Amusement Corporation and the name changed to the Embassy Theater. It was a movie theater until 1971 when both the theater and the hotel were in danger of destruction by a wrecking ball. Over the last 30 years, the theater and hotel have been protected by the community. Renovation is a continuous process. Volunteers see a deceased maintenance man roaming the theater at all hours.

## Ft. Wayne (Town)
**Fort Wayne:** Off I-69

All of Fort Wayne (or most of it) is built on Indian grounds. Many people think that Fort Wayne is haunted because of the ancient burial grounds and just being in old places downtown makes some people feel a presence.

## Greenlawn Cemetery
**Fort Wayne:** Covington Road east of I-69

Floating orbs appear in the cemetery in front of visitors and in photos.

## History Center
*(aka Old Jail)*
**Fort Wayne:** 302 E. Berry St.

Built in 1913, this building has been a city hall, a jail and a fire station. As it is under restoration, many employees have had paranormal experiences. The basement seems to have strange smells around it. Visitors report apparitions of an old man, orbs and transparent children. Some locals believe the basement was used as a morgue. A murderer haunts the old jail, walking through the halls and touching visitors on the neck. Noises like metal on metal are heard as well.

## Jehl Park
**Fort Wayne:** West end of Bohnke Dr.
*(aka Swinger's Grave)*

A girl was strangled by the chain of a swing. If you swing at midnight at Jehl Park, she pushes you off.

## Knee House
**Fort Wayne:** Between Hanna, Warfield, and John Streets and US 27
*(aka Cement House; aka White's/Whites/Whities Mansion)*
*(Razed in 1988)*

The home was built during WWII and construction was halted by the family when the sons went to war. The man built the house for his invalid wife, including a checkerboard pattern in the front entry of the home. He built ramps for her wheelchair. Before he could finish it, she died in 1951. He left the house unfinished because he didn't have the money to continue. The invalid wife walks the home with a light or a candle.

## Lakeside Park Neighborhood
**Fort Wayne:** 1401 Lake Ave.

Located near a lake, this neighborhood was Native American land used for unnamed purposes. The land was also part of an amusement park with canals and a dance hall. Residents hear strange sounds and see apparitions in their homes.

## Leo High School
**Leo:** 14600 Amstutz Rd.

A student died during a stage production and now haunts the auditorium. Lights turn off and on, doors open and close for no reason.

## Main Street Bridge
**Fort Wayne:** Main Street over St. Mary's River

A woman in white walks the bridge but never interacts with people. She's been walking Main Street since the mid-1800s by some accounts and 1903 by others. Sometimes she races over the bridge in a horse drawn carriage.

## Mason Long House
**Fort Wayne:** 922 Columbia Ave.

In 1965 the McCaffrey family moved in– tales of ghosts and all. The home's former life was that of a hotel, casino and drinking establishment. Visitors see misty figures– especially in August.

## New Haven High School and Middle School
**New Haven:** Middle School: 900 Prospect Ave./ High School: 1300 Green Rd.

A ghost of a homeless man walks the tunnel.

## North Side High School
**Fort Wayne:** 475 E. State Blvd.

A Miami chief who tried to stop building in Fort Wayne on the burial site of his tribe roams the halls and grounds of this school. A janitor who died of a heart attack is seen in the basement. A construction worker who died in the building of the school is also seen wandering in the school from the auditorium to the classrooms. The construction worker is often seen by people to warn them of school and personal dangers.

## Old Bryon Health Care Center
*(aka Stairway to Hell)*
**Fort Wayne:** 12101 Lima Rd. (New facility attached to old)

A legend claims that the stairs to be the basement are endless and that no matter how many times you try to go down to the basement, you'll never get there. The ghost of a nurse who died while on duty walks the halls late at night watching over her patients.

## Old Lutheran Hospital
**Fort Wayne:** 3024 Fairfield Ave.
*(Razed, now part of Lutheran Foundation property)*

This old hospital was built on the Ninde homestead property in 1903. Between 1906 and 1975, four additions were made. The current building at 7950 Jefferson Boulevard was built in 1992. The fourth floor of the old hospital had a male ghost that would walk through the silent halls and visit patients.

## Pfeiffer House
**Fort Wayne:** 434 W Wayne St.

Charles and Henrietta Pfeiffer and their children Fred and Marguerite lived in the home. Charles made his money in meat packing and banking. Currently, Fred, who died at almost 100 years of age, inhabits the house still. Pots and pans move, lights turn off and on. Doors open and close. People refuse to go to the attic.

## Snider High School
**Fort Wayne:** 4600 Fairlawn Pass

People hear a girl crying during the day. Legend states that a girl drowned in a pool on the site of the school. She still haunts the building.

## U.S. 20
**Brushy Prairie:** Various areas of US 20

A pale woman in a white gown walks the road. When drivers stop for her, she disappears.

## University of Saint Francis Library
**Fort Wayne:** 2701 Spring St.
*(aka Bass, John H. Mansion, aka Brookside)*

A student committed suicide in the library. Students and staff feel cold spots, hear moans, and see the lights turn off and on around the anniversary of his death. This building is no longer the library, but now houses administrative offices.

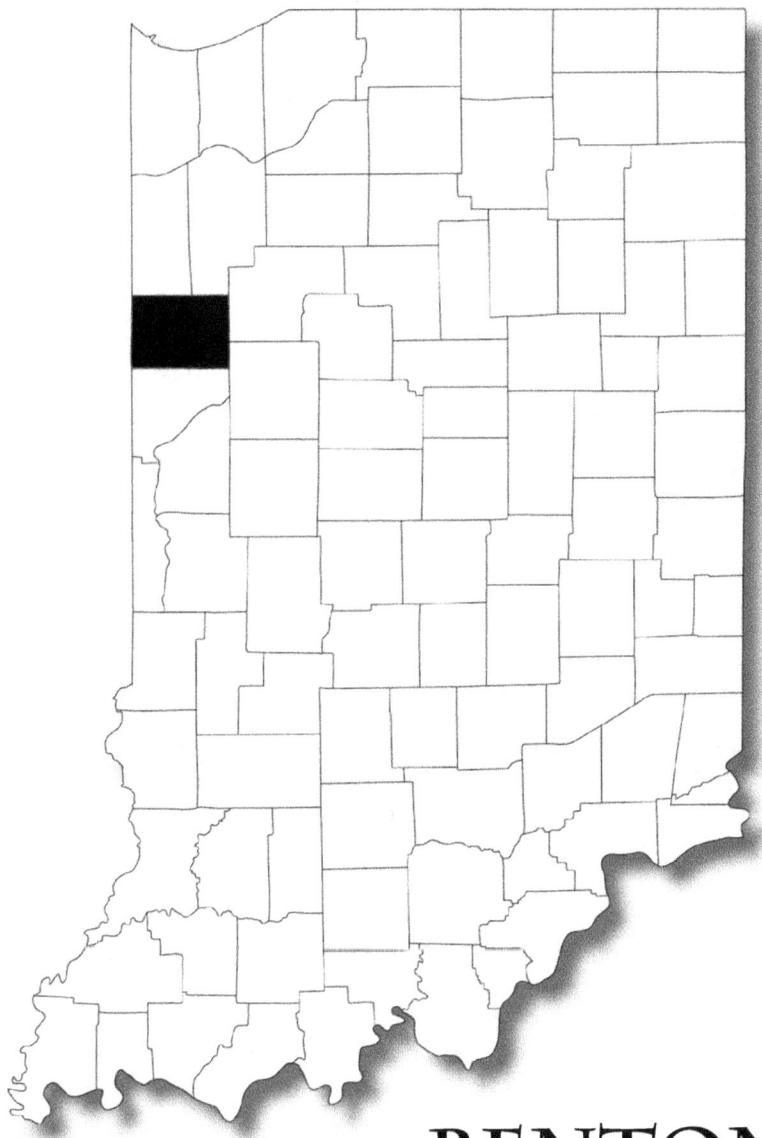

# BENTON
# COUNTY

## Adams Mill / Adams Mill Bridge
**Bolivar (near Cutler):** Between SR 18 and SR 26; .5 miles east of Cutler on CR 50E

While this area has an annual Halloween party with haunted trails, some non-staged paranormal activity also occurs here. Psychics claim the area is a portal that allows spirits to cross between their world and ours. Ghost hunters have captured voices heard calling for help and investigators heard a man say "Are you there, Josie?" Investigators have also taken several pictures in which demons and faces have appeared. EVPs of spirits talking to investigators have also been reported. Also, a woman walks across the water and comes toward you. Down the stairs, into the woods, and across the Adams Mill bridge is a memorial. The woman who walks on the water is rumored to be buried at the memorial.

Built in 1845, this mill was originally called Wildcat Mills because of its location on Wildcat Creek. By 1913, this water-only milling operation was able to produce enough electricity to power Cutler, Sedalia, and Rossville. The bridge was built in 1872. The building is open for tours and features a slanting chimney that starts in a lower level office and continues all the way to the roof of the structure. The ownership and focus of the mill has recently changed, and they may no longer permit investigations to come in and set up equipment.

## Fowler Theatre
**Fowler:** 111 E. 5th St.

Currently under restoration, this 1940s building entertained theater goers for 60 years. Patrons report feelings of being watched and seeing a gray-haired man. Another gray colored man in a fedora is seen in the lobby. Some people believe it is Dick Vlastos, the original owner of the building.

## St. Anthony Cemetery
**Earl Park:** 7048 N. CR 200W

According to legend, this settler cemetery is home to a mist. Sometimes it takes the shape of an 8-9 ft tall, white bearded man who carries a large stick or club. This man is believed to be the ghost of a robber who killed another man for his money. He motions for you to come closer. If you don't approach him, he will come after you with his weapon. Although St. Anthony's Cemetery is not conclusively the cemetery, a man with a white beard has been seen at this location sans gun.

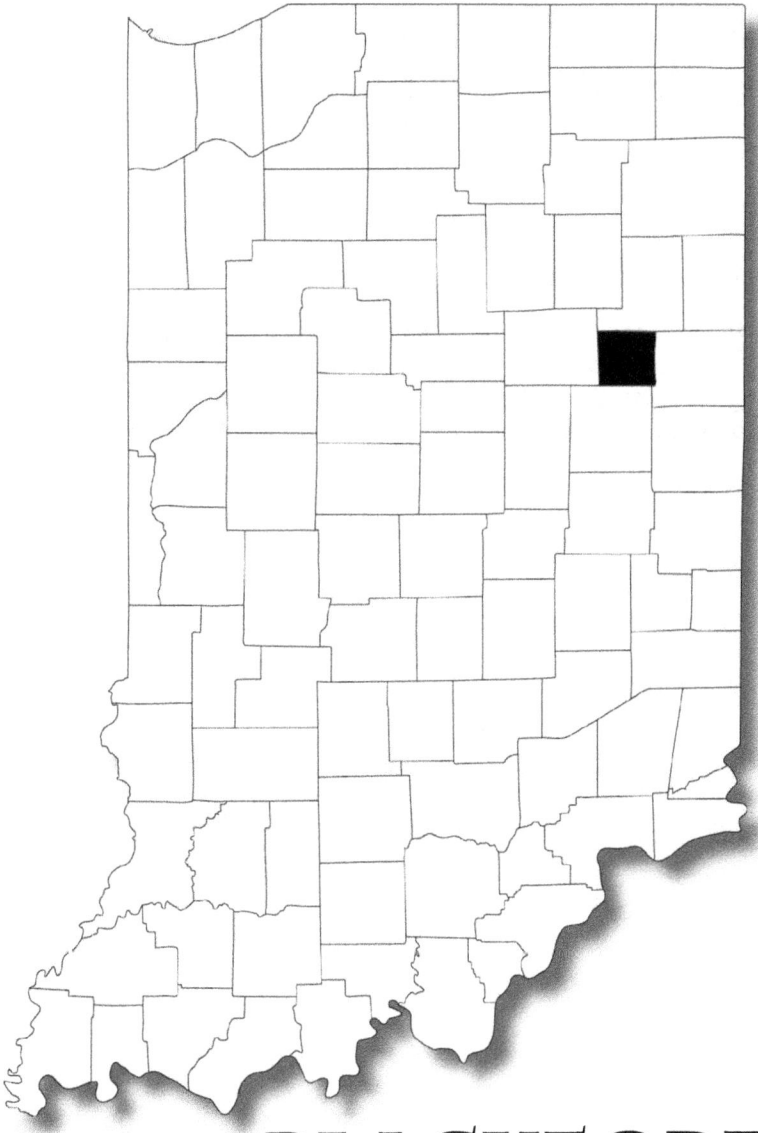

# BLACKFORD COUNTY

## Asbury Chapel
**Montpelier:** 8022 W 1100 S
*(aka United Methodist Church)*

Investigators caught unexplainable bright red, green, and white strands of light. Additionally strange blue, white, red, and green orbs were also captured. Red mists seeped out of the ground. A man who was not part of the investigation was surrounded by red light.

## Montpelier
**Montpelier:** Montpelier town, especially around CR 800 N

A blond bank robber killed in June 1959 haunts the town. He's seen in various spots by law enforcement and private citizens. Usually he is seen trying to break into buildings. His apparition is solid as if he is still among the living. He wears jeans, white tennis shoes, a jean jacket or a leather jacket. When he's chased, he simply disappears. Police have chased this phantom for years.

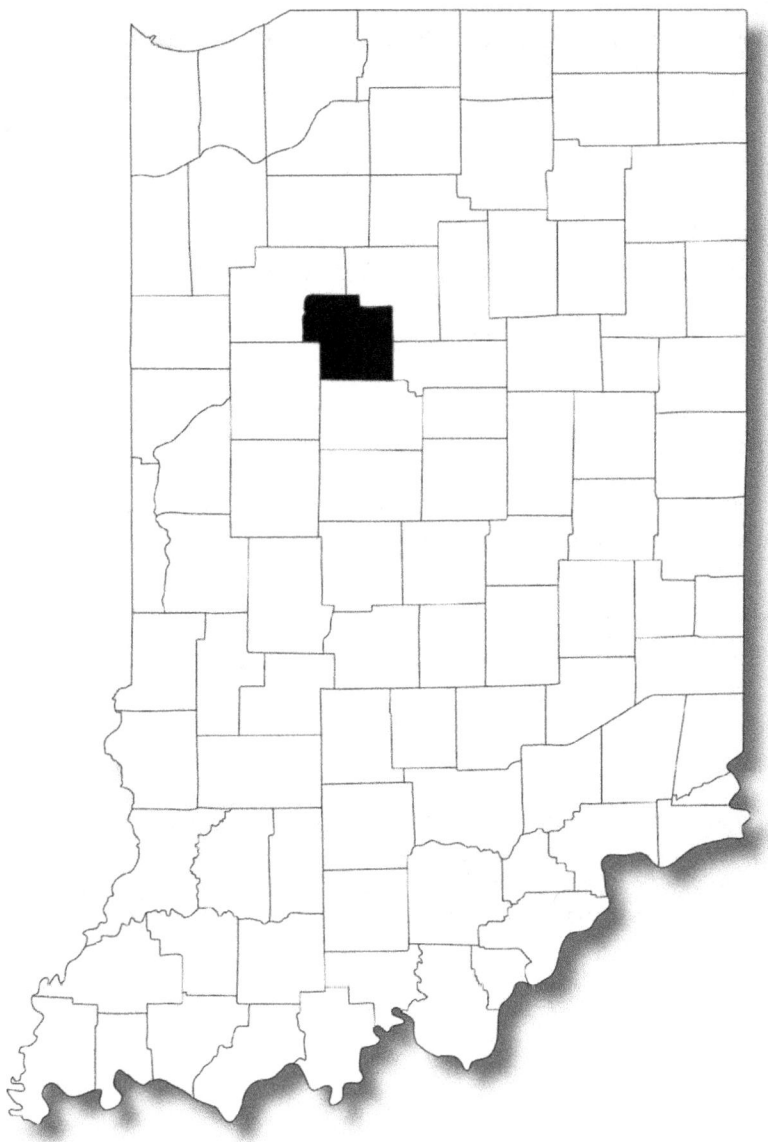

# CARRROL L
# COUNTY

## Ball Hill Cemetery

**Flora:** West of IN 75 on CR W300S between CR S100W and CR S150W

Investigators report several types of mists, colored orbs, and temperature in this pioneer cemetery. During the day, visitors record wisps of white and grey mists. During the evening hours visitors might catch a white or even purple mist.

## Old Flora Cemetery

**Flora:** End of Green Acre Dr. (The road also has a Flora Cemetery sign)

Flashes of light and colored streaks of spirit energy are seen regularly in the cemetery.

## Old Flora School

**Flora:** Main Street east of Division St.

Voices can be heard asking questions if you can hear them. Levitating equipment were witnessed in the school. Locals believe that the people in the old graveyard behind it inhabit the school.

## Old Sycamore Haunted Bridge

**Burlington:** West of US 31 in Kokomo. Take Sycamore Rd. past Malfalfa Rd. (CR N300W). The road will curve to the right onto Sycamore Lane but you want to take Sycamore Rd. (CR W80N). This road eventually curves around and turns into CR W00NS. At CR S440W turn left to get to the bridge.

Drive your car over the bridge, and a phantom white car will chase you to dish out death if it catches you. If you go, be sure to look for the bullet marks on the bridge- legend has it a jealous boyfriend shot at his girlfriend and her new boyfriend, killing them both. The white car appears on any given night. The murdered couple makes appearances in late May and in September.

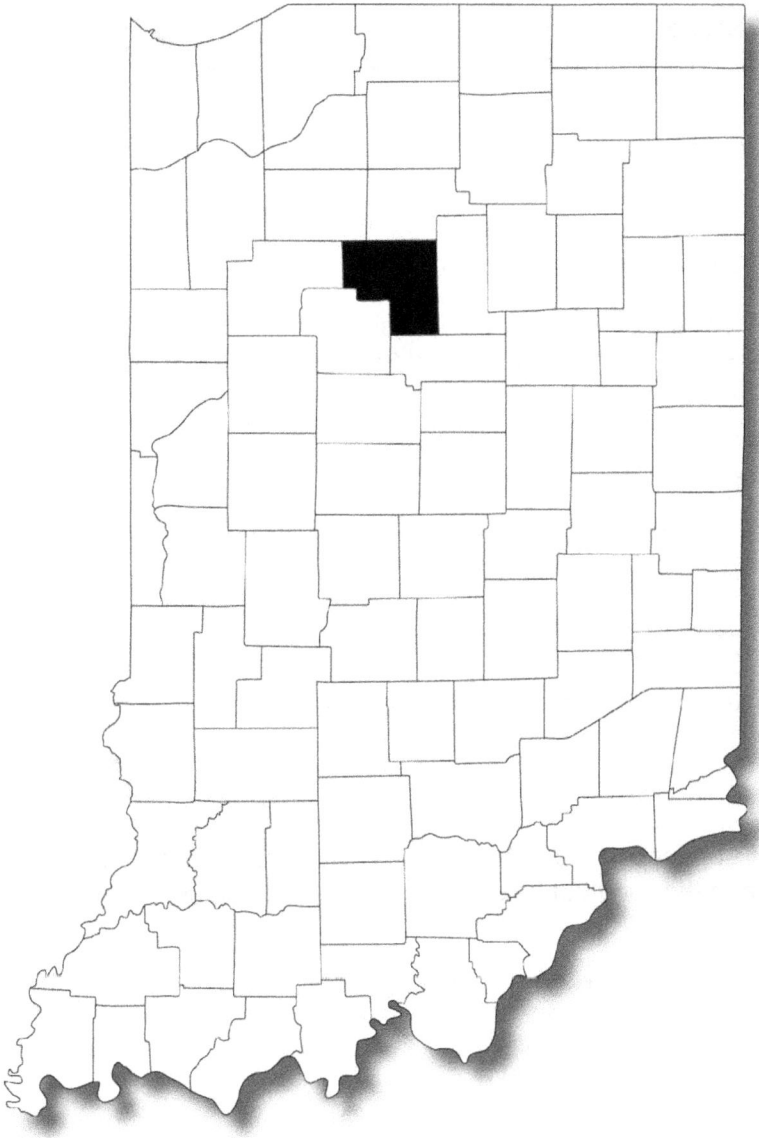

# CASS
# COUNTY

## Longcliff
**Logansport:** 1098 S. SR 25
*(aka Logansport State Hospital- aka Northern Indiana Hospital for the Insane)*

Modeled after Central State, this hospital opened its doors in 1888. In its heyday, the facility had in/out patient facilities, and surgeries. It produced its own food and was a small town onto itself.

## Miami Cemetery
**Adamsboro:** East of S. Eel River Rd. on CR W100N

Two children who are buried here can be seen sitting beside their headstones. Sometimes they call to each other. Other times investigators have reported seeing them run and play tag.

## Mount Hope Cemetery
**Logansport:** 1800 Grant St.

Visitors experience the sounds of horses' hoofbeats and someone whistling.

## Shiloh Church
**Logansport:** 1047 N. CR 350W

A headless horseman haunts the area. If you circle the church and look in the basement windows, you will see an unkempt girl watching you.

## Water Street
**Logansport:** West of Logansport. Take Water St. west (it turns into Delaware Rd.) The pond is on the left side of the road between Holland St. and Kiesling Rd.
*(aka Delaware Rd. swimming hole)*

This man-made pond is used by local kids for swimming. At one time, a child drowned in the pond. Several people report seeing a transparent little boy and little girl walking next to the pond and running around it, giggling. However, when the visitors approached, the children disappeared.

# DEKALB COUNTY

## Abandoned farm
**Butler:** CR 75A north of SR 46 second curve before CR 42. Overgrown but a small path can be see back to the ruins. House has collapsed and may be unsafe. Close to Land of Moses/Gypsies Hill.
*(See Land of Moses/Gypsy Hill, Butler, DeKalb Co.)*


Shadow figures cross the road in front of cars and shape shift in the night air. Disembodied voices cry for help nightly. In the home, visitors are terrified by growling noises. A smell of rotting meat permeates the building.

One investigator walked through the backyard and heard "the most unholy laughter I've ever heard". Legend of this land is that two brothers lived on the property with their mother. One brother killed the other, and the mother hung herself in abject grief from a large oak tree in the back yard. Some visitors believe the sound of the rope is heard swinging from the tree and can be seen during the day and night.


## Auburn Cord Duesenberg Museum
**Auburn:** 1600 S. Wayne St.

Mysterious footsteps and the smell of cigars haunt this building. The lights turn on and off by themselves. One staff member shut all the lights off and closed up the museum. Walking to the parking lot, the worker noticed the light in a former office was on. The worker went back into the museum and turned the light off. The next day, the museum staff received notice that the wife of the man who used to work in the office had died the previous evening.

Other interesting facts:
- Auburn Automobile Co. produced a model 666, known as "Satan's car."
- Race car driver, Scott Brayton donated a fully restored Italian Cisitalia. Weeks later, he died in a crash at the Indianapolis Motor Speedway.
- One of the cars donated to the museum is said to have been given to a daughter by her father. She later died in it.


## Land of Moses
**Butler:** South of US 6 at CR 28 and CR 79.
*(aka Gypsy Hill)*
*(See Abandoned Farm, Butler, DeKalb Co.)*

Gypsies used to make camp here. According to a local legend, the gypsies kidnapped and raped a farmer's daughter, although it isn't clear if she died. Her father and other farmers killed the gypsies in retaliation. Over the next decade each farmer who participated was brutally killed with an axe. The spirits of the gypsies and farmers are said to haunt the area.

Investigations have uncovered EVPs that sound like screams and fighting. Moans and wails are also heard. Ethnic music has also been recorded when no music was playing at the time.

# ELKHART
# COUNTY

## Bristol Opera House
**Bristol:** 210 Vistula St.
*(aka Elkhart Civic Theater)*

This 100+ year old building is haunted by Percy, who seems to like the name Percival better. Legend has two stories about Percy. As the stories go, either he was a woodworker who squatted at the building with his family during the depression or his home burned by fire or he was allowed to live in the building. Staying in the lower levels of the theatre, he loves to appear to women (although he does appear to men). He likes to watch the action in the theatre. He has been known to help with set construction, and to hide tools. According to psychics and investigators, a little girl named Beth looks through the curtains on stage. A woman named Helen protects the theater. Two other spirits, Frank and Tad, have been identified as pranksters. Sometimes these spirits levitate objects. Some people feel taps on their shoulders in the theatre seats and costume room. Investigators have collected pictures with orbs and shadows and recordings of EVPs.

## Cable Line Road
**Jamestown:** Near Jamestown (or Jimtown) (CR 26)

A troll lives under the bridge. If your car stalls on it, the troll will drag you under the bridge and kill you. At times, fog is seen at this location when conditions are right for it. Other mythical like creatures are seen dancing off the road nearby.

In the 1960s a motorcycle rider was killed when his bike crashed into a tree. The tree was said to bleed every year. In September 1999 a woman died at this same location when her car slammed into a telephone pole.

## County Road 18
**Middlebury:** CR 18

An Amish man who was hit and killed by a car is seen walking along the road, trying to return home. A man on a motorcycle was also killed on this road and is seen riding his bike.

## The Cross on Mill Stone
**Bristol:** The Bonneyville Mill, in the Bonneyville Mill Park on CR 8, just outside Bristol, Indiana is a popular tourist destination.

Home to the oldest operating gristmill in Indiana, this mill has a colorful history. Edward Bonney started the mill and had somewhat of a checkered past, dabbling in anything that was guaranteed to make him money. When he sold it and moved away, the mill became a place for the town to gather and talk. One child was killed when he fell in the inner workings of the mill and was crushed.

Legend states that a cross appears on the original stone at the mill (although some say it is a leveling mark). The boy has been heard and seen in the rafters of the building, laughing.

## Goshen College–Umble Center
**Elkhart:** 1700 S. Main St.

The Umble Center, built in 1978, was named after John S. Umble. His wife Alice haunts the center. She prefers the fly loft and the catwalk, making walking and creaking sounds. She also likes to play with the lights, dimming them at her whim.

## Haunted Farm
**Elkhart:** 23128 CR 28

Electronic issues occur in this house. Unplugged radios play music, and the TV changes channels alone. Lights turn off and off without help. A mirror in the home is said to show people from your past who have died. Blankets are pulled from sleepers. Misty apparitions are also reported. One apparition is said to wave at you and you can hear a voice faintly as if from a distance.

## Jackson Cemetery
**New Paris:** West of US 33, north of Elkhart St. (CR 44)

Apparitions of African Americans are said to walk the road and haunt the cemetery. So far, no reasons have been found for these apparitions. It is an active cemetery with hours from 7am to 7pm.

## Oakridge Cemetery
**Elkhart:** Grave is at back of cemetery. Bordered by N. First St., River Ave., N. Indiana Ave. and W. Wilden Ave.
*(aka Michael Bashor's Grave)*

Michael Bashor, founder of Bashor's Children home was a mason. A statue at the grave of Michael Bashor cries tears of blood. At night, a woman in a long wispy see-through white dress walks through the cemetery and stops at Bashor's grave. This same woman can be heard weeping. People have noticed figures darting among the graves at night- although this could be animals or teenagers who frequently trespass at night.

## Old Elkhart Hospital
**Elkhart:** 126 N. Clark St.

Opened in 1899, the hospital was used until 1914 when the community built larger structure. Later, it became an apartment building where doctors still walk the halls. Some people have reported a stern nurse in a white dress and cap. Crying and whimpering are frequently heard.

*(Note: Nursing was not an official profession as we know it today until 1921, well after the time this hospital was no longer in use.)*

## Ruthmere House Museum

**Elkhart:** 307 W. High St.

AR Beardsley built the home and was the president of the Muzzy Starch Company. He and his wife, Elizabeth, died in 1924. Items levitate to different rooms, lights go on and off and alarms sound for no reason. Elizabeth loved to entertain and is believed to be the one haunting the museum.

## Stagecoach Inn Bed and Breakfast

**Goshen:** 66063 US 33

Lights come on at night without anyone turning them on. A white mist is seen in the building. Spirits have also been seen peeking around doors.

## Union Cemetery

**Elkhart:** CR 11 and CR 50

The gravestone of Irwin Yoders weeps because of all the vandalism in the cemetery.

## Winchester Mansion

**Elkhart:** 529 S. Second St.

Nellie (Knickerbocker) Winchester lived the life of a society girl and later matron. She kept her family's plot in Grace Lawn Cemetery pristine and became obsessed with her own arrangements. She eventually bought a solid copper coffin. Nellie died in her home in 1947. Although she came from money, her estate was meager at her death, amounting to about $11,000. Items in the home move and once, the back of a grandfather clock fell out. Office workers have experienced cold spots, and unexplained cool breezes. They have also heard footsteps in the empty building.
It is now a multipurpose building.

# FULTON
# COUNTY

## Antioch Cemetery

**Rochester:** West of SR 25 on CR S75W

A man in a dark colored suit holding flowers haunts this cemetery. He is often seen kneeling at various graves on foggy nights between 12-1am. Shadow people fly over and around vehicles. If you walk the cemetery at night, these shadows follow you around the cemetery.

## Deadmans College School and Cemetery

**Rochester:** South of SR 110 at the corner of CR N500W and CR W700N
*(often misspelled Dead Man's College)*

This one room pre-1875 school building is on the site of a family cemetery. This location is linked to Prill School because "Sister Sarah's (McIntire)" baby was buried at this site. In the evening and early morning, people visiting this site hear children playing and they'll ask you to join them. People also see children running in the yard as well.

*(See Prill School entry, Rochester, Fulton Co.)*

## Earl's Tree Cemetery

**Rochester:** Off SR 25 on CR 300S

A boy named Earl speaks to you about the tree next to his grave.

## Fulton Cemetery

**Fulton:** SR 25 between CR E700S and CR E600S

A couple that died in a car accident were buried together around 1967. Many stabbings and shootings have occurred in the area. Investigators have captured mists, orbs and EVPs of people talking. One EVP has a group of unseen people talking. Someone pipes up and asks "If we ask, do you think they'll go?" Also, some visitors have reported an apparition of a man whose grave was desecrated.

## Olson Road

**Rochester:** On Olson Road between Old and New US 31
*(aka Slaughterhouse Rd.)*

The old slaughterhouse is part of what people consider to be a time warp. When you drive by, some people have claimed that this building disappears. Even if you try to walk to it, you still can't find it.

## Prill School

**Rochester:** 500 W. Seventh St.

Sister Sarah taught at the school and died (depending on the source, it ranges from rape and murder to poison to disease). Sister Sarah haunts the school. If you visit on a night of a full moon, her ghost walks the grounds, especially next to the tree in the yard. If you put a question on a slip of paper and leave it, she will give you answers.

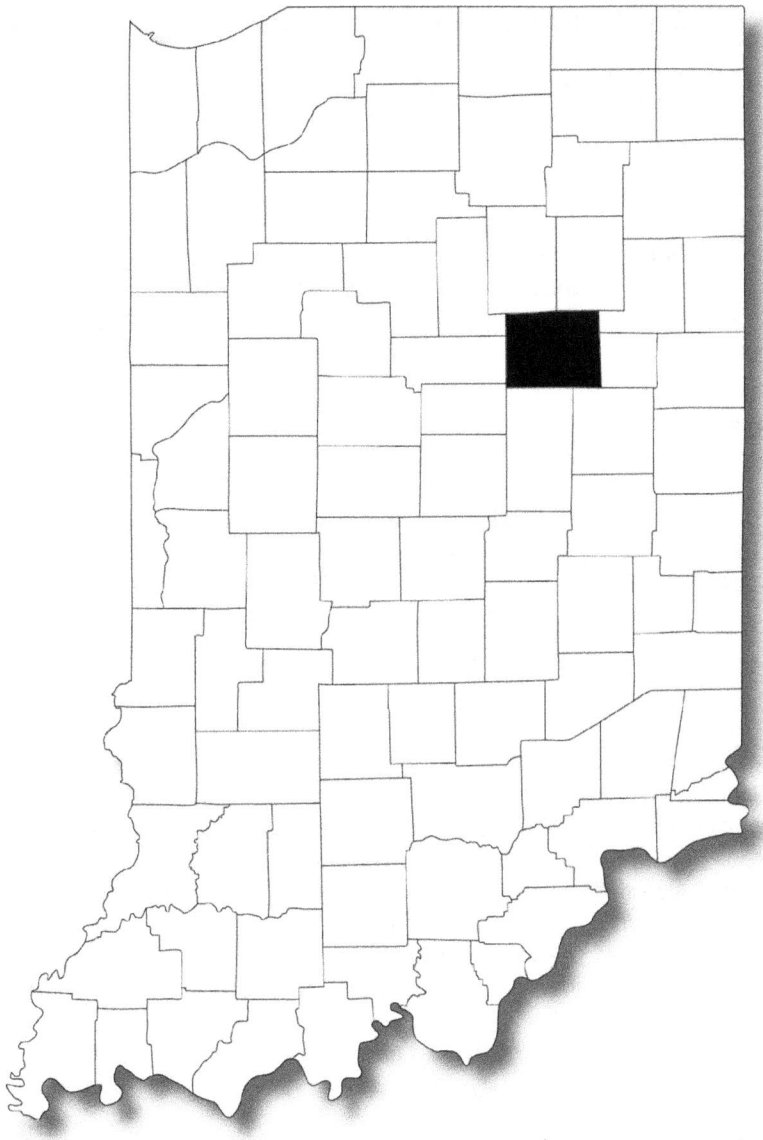

# GRANT
# COUNTY

## 10th Street Bridge

**Gas City:** Take 10th Street north from US 35/ SR 22. It will be the bridge over Walnut Creek.

**Jonesboro:** Take 10th Street east. It is the bridge over the Mississinewa River. (10th St. turns into West L St.)

A worker died on the bridge. You can hear his screams asking for help.

*Much controversy surrounds whether or not this bridge is actually in Gas City or Jonesboro. Both 10th Streets have a bridge. From the time the author spent in the Grant County area with family over the years, her experience has been that it is the Jonesboro Bridge. However, Readers, you be the final judge. Perhaps they both have stories to tell.*

## 1524 Marion Avenue

**Marion:** 1524 Marion Ave.

An older man who owned this home likes to play pranks on people who rent the home. He hides items, and turn the television on and off. His loud booming laughter can be heard throughout the home. His wife is around as well, most often with the smell of her favorite powder emanating from the bathroom. Both of them are heard in the kitchen playing cards.

## Bennett High School

**Marion:** 1009 Kem Rd.

*(aka St. Paul Catholic School)*

This now defunct high school is home to an assorted lot of ghosts.

- Gym Balcony: The ghost of a former teacher roams the hall. She was fired for getting divorced and killed herself.
- Upstairs girls' bathroom: Faucets turn on and off at random. Many times, visitors hear someone pushing a mop bucket although no one is around. One other story is about a girl in the 1980s having aborted her baby in the restroom and flushing the baby and birth material down the toilet.
- Coach's Room (West side of Gym): Rumor has it that a former coach molested a student in this location. Although the girl survived, the vibration of the past remains and her muffled sobs are heard in the late evening. A variation of this story is that a former priest molested a young male student here.
- Cafeteria: Many students report a mischievous ghost of a former student. He appears as a grey mist.. He throws cafeteria trays and trips people.

## Charles Road

**Marion:** West of N. Bethlehem Rd. and East of SR 9/109/37

A whole pioneer family was decapitated. Today the family's screams are heard and you can hear the wagon traveling down the road. Sometimes a headless man or woman is seen walking on the road.

## Converse Elementary School
**Converse:** 600 East Walnut St.

A 49 year old woman hung herself from the flag pole. Staff members and locals say that at night, you can see her swinging from the pole and standing on the ground crying.

## The Hostess House
**Marion:** 723 W. 4th St.
*(aka The Sleeping House)*

An older woman was killed in the house. Today you can see her shadowy figure on her balcony. She also haunts the room where she slept. Sometimes she interacts with people to ask them to take care of the house. Sometimes she is seen walking in the hallway, she is also seen in an upstairs window. Some people believe it is the ghost of a housekeeper. Others believe it is Peggy "Lillian" Wilson, for whom the home was built.

## Israel Jenkins Farm
**Marion:** 7453 E 400 S (on Club Run course)
*(aka Walnut Creek Club Run; aka The Elms)*

The Jenkins were Quakers who settled in Marion in 1839 and were active in the Underground Railroad. Footsteps are heard, lights turn on and off. Doors open and close, and there are shadow figures on stairs walking up to the attic and the attic door opens when no one is seen. A young man stares out of the attic window.

## J.C. Knight School
**Jonesboro:** 12th and Main Streets

A janitor hung himself in the gym and a cheerleader was murdered in the building. You can see white lights dancing inside the school. Sometimes they are red lights or turn red.

## Marion National Cemetery – VA Medical Center
**Marion:** 1700 East 38th Street

This cemetery and VA medical center are haunted by various apparitions of men and woman. Some are believed to be patients and other people who worked there. Some of the patients report watching deceased soldiers walk on the grounds at night and in the corridors of the hospital.

## Mason's Bridge
**Gas City:** CR 222 to CR 400 E

In the 1940s a husband and wife got into an argument and he cut off her head at the bridge. Feeling guilty, he hung himself in the house. Two people are seen running down the hill- one with an axe. They replay the event in which you can hear screaming and crying, and the thud of the head as it hits the bridge, screams and crying. The woman is said to roam the banks looking for her head.

## Old East School
**Upland:** S. 4th St.; south of SR 35/SR 22

The merry-go-round spins by itself and you can hear children laughing.

*(Note: The merry-go-round is long gone.)*

## Park Cemetery
### Fairmount: CR S150E south of CR E800S

In the center point of four trees, you feel that someone is touching you. Movie star, James Dean has also been seen at his grave looking down at it. There is also a spot in the cemetery with four trees surrounding it that. If you stand in the middle of them, you may feel someone touching you.

## Scott Opera House
**Fairmount:** 45 Downtown Plaza
*(aka Fairmont Opera House)*

Students using the 120-year old building for band rehearsal have experienced lights turning on and off and items moving from one place to another by unseen hands. People have been locked in rooms.

## Spook's Corner
**Upland:** West of SR 26 on CR E825S where it curves by the river.

In the 1970s a bus load of kids was supposed to have been killed in the rushing river when it careened off the road. The legend states there is a bus in a cemetery nearby, although there are no documented graveyards around. Additionally, if you go over the "iron bridge" children will try to push you off it. The bridge that is currently on this road is not iron, it is guardrails and blacktop.

## Sweetser (town)
**Sweetser:** On SR 18 west of Marion and east of SR 13

In the late 1960s, child saw a Native American group outside at the family's old well on the property. The girl saw the Native Americans and they saw her, but when the girl told her mother, she couldn't see what her daughter saw. Others throughout the town also reported the Native Americans. They are spotted most often wearing buckskin pants and traveling in a group.

## Woodcarver Building
**Converse:** 101 S. Jefferson St.
*(aka Eastern Woodland Carvers Building; aka Odd Fellows; aka IOOF Converse; aka AJ Fisher building)*

Throughout its history, the second floor used to be a doctor's office, a KKK office, and storeroom. Visitors and investigators hear a piano playing childlike songs on the second floor. People have been choked on this floor after automatic writing events. Orbs take shape on the stairway leading to this floor. People have been pushed from the stairs. A full apparition crosses from one side of this floor to the other side.

On the first floor an apparition walks through the room without interacting with visitors. In all areas of the building electronic malfunctions occur and visitors hear footsteps. Cell phones and batteries drain. People have also been locked in the building from the latch on the outside. Legend states tunnels exist under the building and throughout Converse.

On the third floor, the KKK used to meet. Investigators have reported unexplained EMF readings and shadow figures. Light fixtures swing without reason.

# HUNTINGTON COUNTY

## Batson Cemetery

**Warren:** SR 3 off of Willow Rd.

*(aka 13 Graves)*

The remnants of an old limestone walkway have been the source of many legends at this cemetery. Some believe the limestone is not a walkway but unnamed graves. If you count them walking one direction, they will number 13. If you count the other way, they number 12. Another legend of this place is that an old man used to be caretaker of a blind school that was torn down years ago. As the children were scared of ghosts coming out of the cemetery, he used to go into the cemetery where the children could see him. He told the kids he'd keep anything from coming to get them at night. One night while sitting in the cemetery, the man died of a heart attack. One of the children in the school said he came to her and asked her to get someone to take care of his body. He is buried in the cemetery. Today, people have seen his apparition as well as captured orbs and streaks of light.

One other story concerns the area is a house (some people say it was the blind school). Disease swept through the building and killed many people. They were all buried together and concrete was poured over them. The building was burned to the ground

## Browns Corners
**Markle:** West of I-69 at CR S200E and CR E100S

This area is home to creatures some might be considered Bigfoot. One creature seen at the location is brown and similar in shape to a human. Some reports put this creature at about 9 ft. while others say it is more around 6 feet. Another creature that is pale in comparison has been seen is estimated at 4-7 feet in height. These creatures have been seen day and night in the area and have been seen for at least the last 50 years. Many people have attempted to speak to the creatures but when they speak to it, the creature runs away. People who have pursued it describe a wail, a scream similar to an animal that has been caught in a bear trap.

Local legends say that some of the Indiana State Police have gone missing (some say due to KKK activity, others say the creature got them) and only their uniforms were found- neatly folded in a pile. No conclusive proof of this has been discovered. A story has been circulating about a couple that went out to the area and went into the woods. When they came back to the car, one of their windows was shattered, the car was turned on (although the key was not in it) and a rather large handprint had been melted into their dashboard.

## Canal House

**Roanoake:** E. of Roanoake on US 24. Remnants of Wabash and Erie canal 1.7 miles east

Lorenzo "Van" VanBecker had a farm here. He tried to increase his wealth in many ways- one being a lodging house. He hired Mariah Heddwick, a woman suspected of being a witch. When Van's wife fell ill, Mariah said she could help her. Instead of being helped, Van's wife died. From that point on, someone has been heard calling out for help.

Today, this area has a number of bright lights that are seen flitting through the trees.

## Forks of the Wabash
**Huntington:** Forks of the Wabash

A house along this area of the Wabash belonged to Chief Richardsville. At one time it was remodeled adding a door that led from the Chief's quarters to the servant's rooms. In this area, cold breezes and temperatures are felt. Many people feel that the Chief or his staff are still in the home. Some believe that they've seen "whisps of the spirits" of those who still roam the area.

## Horace Mann School
**Huntington:** 521 William St., Apt. 307

This school is now apartments but the former visitors haven't left- yet. Apparitions of children and adults have been seen. One EVP seems to have caught someone talking about homework.

## Huntington College
**Huntington:** 2303 College Ave.

A woman shrouded in black (or white- depending on the account) is seen gliding through the PE Recreation center. More men see her, but women have seen her as well. The lights in this building turn on and off without human help and the faucets turn on by themselves. The toilets flush seemingly spontaneously.

## Mt. Etna (town)
**Mt. Etna (town):** East of SR 9 on SR 124

Mt. Etna was settled by German immigrants and named after a Sicilian volcano. Today, it is a partial reservoir and a mecca for hunters and fishermen. The Salamonie Reservoir runs over the northern section of this town. The reservoir was originally built to control flooding in the Upper Wabash River Basin (Mt. Etna) as well as relieve flooding along the lower Wabash and Ohio rivers (southern Indiana). On the northern end of the town a sign reads, "Road ends in water." To create the reservoir, Mt. Etna cemetery was relocate. With the coming of the reservoir, residents no longer had a direct route to the county seat.

Many people believe that the unhappiness in this town caused by the coming of the reservoir and also the relocation of the cemetery is the source for the negative energy and apparitions that are seen in the area.

## Monument City
**Monument City remains:** Take W Monument City Rd. east of CR S700W. It takes you very close to the reservoir. GPS coordinates: 40.763736, -85.592122
**Monument City Memorial Cemetery:** CR S800W just south of CR W250S

This town was flooded in 1965 to create the Salamonie reservoir. Some visitors report when the reservoir is low, ruins of this city can be seen, and the phantom sound of the old church bell can often be heard. The Monument City Memorial

Cemetery was moved. It houses the town's namesake monument and includes a memorial to Polk township residents who lost their lives in the Civil War. The cemetery was moved around 1965 as well to make room for the reservoir. As a result, many people including psychics believe that this area of the reservoir and the new cemetery hold negative energy from the disturbance of both the cemetery and the town.

## Polk Road

**Huntington:** Polk Rd.

A woman died on train track that used to run through here. Today, as you drive down this road, a woman who looks as if she'd been caught in the rain will stumble down the street. When you approach, she disappears or she will get into the car and tell you how she died. Some accounts say she leaves bloody handprints on your car.

## Salamonie River State Forest

**Andrews:** The park office address is Salamonie River State Forest, 9214 West-Lost Bridge. Its main access in Wabash County is SR 524 and CR 100S.
*(aka Wabash County State Forest)*

Near the Salamonie Reservoir, black shadows have been seen running through the forest. Strange lights also have been known to appear, along with a foul odor. Witnesses have even claimed to see wolf-like creatures wandering about the forest. Hikers say that time seems to stand still while hiking and the trails appear to shift, causing some unlucky people to be lost.

A phantom church bell rings and someone dies. The smell of death and long, dark shadows that seem to follow visitors along the Reservoir. Lights from unexplained sources are seen. Apparitions of wolves are frequently seen and some visitors are chased by them. Visitors sense being watched and some visitors have become lost on trails citing a sense of being lost in a space warp/time shift.

## Warrick Hotel

**Huntington:** 511 N. Jefferson St.

Although the current building is home to a haunted house, some people believe the story behind the building. As the story goes, the original hotel burnt down on October 13, 1904 killing 302 people including members of a circus. Unexplained noises and apparitions are heard and seen. Some people believe that visitors to the area have disappeared and were found babbling incoherently at Devil's Backbone or have not been found at all. Rumors persist, despite a lack of evidence supporting this story.

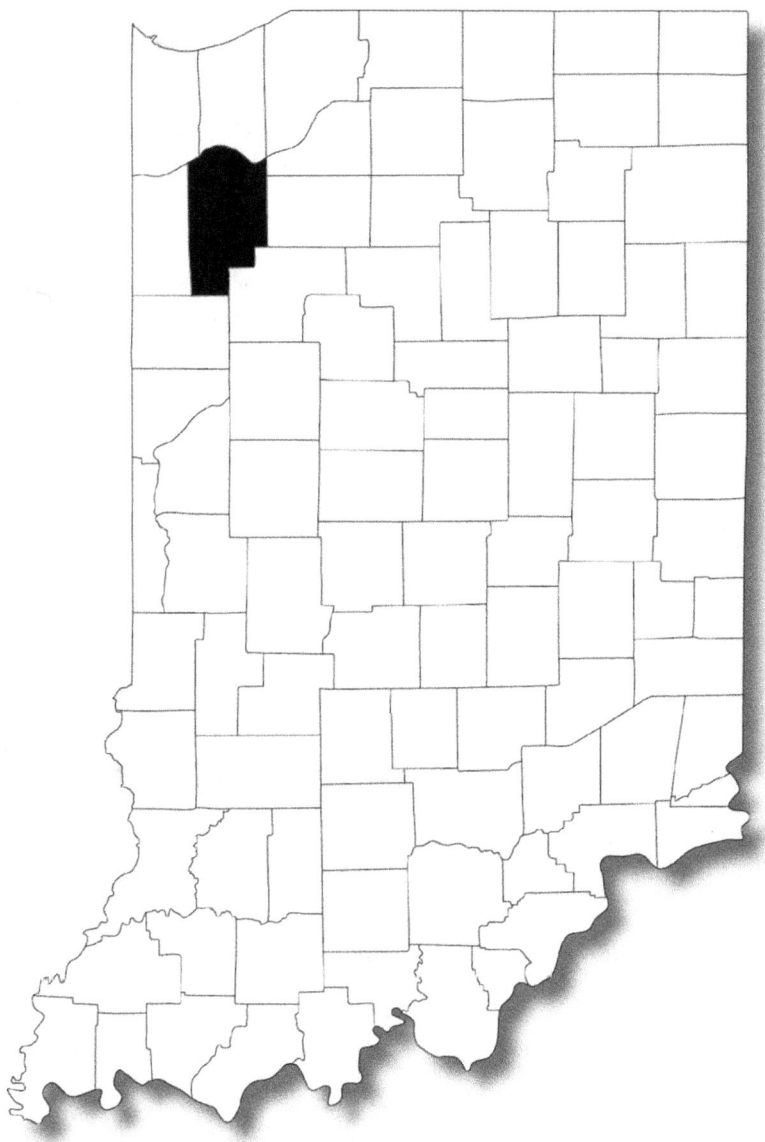

# JASPER
# COUNTY

## Asphaltum

**Asphaltum:** Between CR N250E and CR N300E on CR 600N.

At one time, this town was home to American Lubricating and Refining Company. Many oil wells scattered the countryside, and unfortunately the wells were shallow. During its heyday, according to some sources, Asphaltum was filled with many saloons and brothels. Railroaders were said to have come to Asphaltum to party then leave on the same train that brought them. Little evidence of that decadent life exists today. All that remains are a couple homes, possibly some oil tanks, and a few abandoned oil wells.

The wooded areas to the south of the former town are said to hold its remains, including its many spirits. A solid apparition of woman in a dark blue gown is said to run through the trees as if pursued by someone. A look of extreme terror covers her face. Some visitors have reported hearing the sound of two sets of footfalls, presumably the woman's and her pursuer's. Some investigators have speculated that she is a prostitute trying to escape from one of her customers, or perhaps even her employer.

## Memory Gardens

**Rensselaer:** 250 N. McKinley Ave.

Reportedly a statue at back of cemetery moves, follows and stares at you.

## Moody's Light

**Rensselaer:** CR 230E to Meridian Rd.

A phantom light is seen making its way through the farm fields and is said to change color and size.

*(See also Moody's Light, Francesville, Pulaski Co.)*

## St. Joseph's College

**Rensselaer:** St. Joseph has a map of the campus on its website.

- Aquinas Hall: This is the supposed site of exorcism. No one at the school wants to speak of it.
- Drexel Hall: Now restricted and on the list of Indiana's most Endangered Landmarks. Voices are heard when no one is around.
- Dwenger Hall: Demons roam the halls. Lights are seen by people outside.
- Hallas Hall: A young woman delivered a baby in this building and it died. You can hear the baby cry.
- Theater: A priest hung himself in the theater after an unsucessful exorcism gone badly. People see shadows on the catwalk. When the lights are off, they see the outline of a white figure dangling from it. Doors open and close without reason and the stage is full of cold spots.

## Smith Cemetery

**Rensselaer:** Corner of Surrey Rd. and CR 100

*(aka Twin Cemeteries)*

A Romeo and Juliet scene plays out here. The couple killed themselves, and wanted to be buried side-by-side. Instead the families buried them apart. Now they reappear to attempt to reunite. If you park in front of the two cemeteries, you will see a dark haired woman and a man in a suit walk across the road. Also, your car may die. People who are profanity have been attacked.

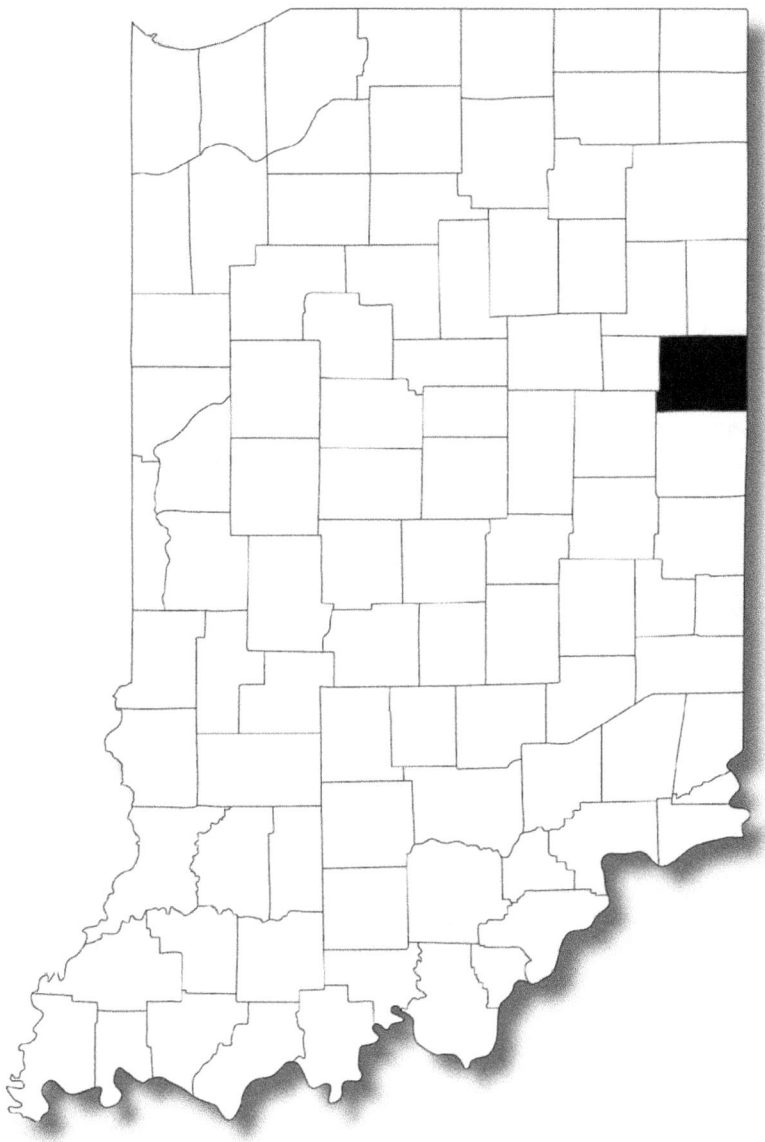

# JAY
# COUNTY

## Adams House

**Portland:** 520 E. High St.

*(aka Coldren's House)*

This home was built in 1894 by David L. Adams. Today, the owners report paranormal activity. Investigators report feeling welcomed by the home.

## Blood Road

**Dunkirk:** CR 700 just off Eaton Pike

Driving down this road, you'll feel a bump and see a trail of blood. The legend goes that a man killed his wife and put her body in his car. When he hit the bump in the road, her body fell out and it was dragged down the road. Another story is that a farmer and his son frequently traveled the road. The boy would jump out of the truck while it was moving so one day his dad chained him to the truck. When he jumped again, he was dragged over two miles. Heading west you will see nothing on the road, but if you go east, you will see blood on the road. Supposedly the home where they lived (unknown location) is very haunted; the boy is buried in the basement.

## Crybaby Bridge

**Redkey:** On IN 1 at CR W825N

Supposedly a school bus full of Girl Scouts went over the bridge, and now you can hear them crying down there. If you stop on the bridge and turn off your car, it might not start again.

## Gray Hotel

**Redkey:** 10 High St.

Many entities of men and women are in this former hotel. From the basement to the top floor, items are manipulated; lights turn on and off, footsteps are heard. Visitors are touched by cold, moist hands. People are plagued with physical symptoms as well. Dizziness, upset stomachs and feeling hot and cold have been reported. A barber shop was once located in the hotel. Its owner was killed near the railroad tracks next to the building. Fairies, pixies and other mythological creatures have also been reported.

## Laughing Scarecrow

**New Corydon:** SR 116 west of CR N750E

From September to November, an apparition of a scarecrow appears in the woods to the west of SR 116. It laughs and screams at people.

## Little Salamonia Cemetery
**Portland:** Boundary Pike Road and CR 300S.

*(aka Boundary Pike Road)*

A boy and his mom died on this road. They are buried in the cemetery. They come out at night and stand in front of your car. If you keep driving towards them, they disappear at the last minute.

## New Corydon
**New Corydon:** SR 116 west of CR N750E. The devil creature is seen west of CR N700E along the banks of the Wabash River.

Strange lights dance on the country roads around this area. Additionally, a feeling of dread pervades the area. Investigators report a creature described as a hump-backed devil with hoofed feet.

## Old Portland High School
**Portland:** It was turned into a middle school and torn down in 2002.

A janitor fell off a ladder killing himself and the person holding the ladder. Cold spots and apparitions of the janitor are experienced.

## Pringley Cemetery
**Portland:** West of US 27 on CR 500N, go north on N. Liberty Rd. After the sharp left turn, you'll see a bridge. Cross the bridge and go north to the cemetery.

Shadow figures carrying lights go up to the cemetery and disappear. They will also follow you back down the hill. Investigators report these lights as guiding lights. Some investigators believe they are more sinister in nature.

## Shoestring Tree
**Redkey:** Unknown

*(aka Shoetree)*

A man was killed and his shoes thrown into a tree. He haunts the area because his killer was never found. According to the legend, he tries to kill you and throw your shoes in the tree.
Another part of the story goes that a man was walking through the woods and found the oak tree, when he looked up, something slit his throat. If you touch the tree, the same fate will happen to you.

## Wentz Cemetery
### Portland: CR W650S

*(aka Cinderella's Grave)*

To the south of the Jay County Conservation Club is a cemetery. Several stories circulate about this place. There is a grave with "Cinderella" written on it. This name supposedly goes with a boy who is buried there. Another version states it is a girl who was abused by her family and died. The people around the area put the stone there with the name Cinderella because they didn't know her name but wanted to give her dignity. Supposedly, when you count the stones going right there are 13 and when you recount left, there are only 11.

# KOSKIUSKO COUNTY

## Barbee Hotel
**Warsaw:** 3620 N. Barbee Rd.

Once a high class hiding spot and retreat for Al Capone and his cronies, this lakeside hotel is now host to a variety of ghosts. Capone stayed in room 301. Visitors and staff have smelled his cigar smoke. In the bar/restaurant, bartenders and visitors have seen several misty figures sitting at booths. When they approach the figures, they simply disappear. In the Gable/Lombard suite, one guest woke up to cigarette smoke and the apparition of Clark Gable sitting at a table smoking a cigarette. As the guest woke his wife, Gable disappeared from sight. Guests and staff hear footsteps on the stairs and several orbs and mists have been captured in pictures.

## Berst House
**Leesburg:** 5677 N. CR 150W
*(aka Green-Stone House)*

Built in 1868 by Titus and Matilda Berst, the building is now home to several ghosts. Two girls have been seen playing, and scared former owners enough that they moved out. A man and a woman are seen in one of the downstairs rooms. A musty odor in the back of the home is often smelled, although no reason for the odor exists.

## Buffalo Street
**Warsaw;** North end of Buffalo St.

George Ininger used to run a hamburger joint in the early 1900s. Today, his spirit is seen at work in his sanitary uniform, walking home.

## Devil's Back Bone
**Warsaw:** SR 25 south of Warsaw

A family in a horse and wagon lost control of the rig. They ended up in the swamp and were sucked under. Visitors hear the wagon, the impact and their screams. Others say they've seen the reenactment of the accident.

## Leesburg Lights
**Leesburg:** Leesburg between North Webster

Mysterious lights follow people. Visitors speculate these lights are no more than house lights or car lights. Others believe they are lights from a UFO or pixie lights.

## Little/Big Barbee Lake
**Warsaw:** Little/Big Barbee Lake

A Native American maiden walks the shores of the lake. At times, she's also seen floating above the water in the full moon light. She seems to be a residual haunting of unknown events in the past.

## Merbrink
**Winona Lake:** 410 Administration Blvd.

Once used for many learning events like the Chautauqua Conference and Bible conferences, Miss Phoebe appears in a white gown on the porch. Dolls and other items move from room to room. Cold spots and breezes are felt. The scent of flowers and incense is detected. Miss Phoebe was also seen napping on a couch by a former resident.

## North Webster Elementary School
**North Webster:** 5475 N. CR 750E

A playful young boy spirit named Daniel (in tan pants and a blue sweater) turns the lights off and on and sits in the library. On the first and second floor, footsteps of a woman in heels walks across the floors. The lockers in hallways open at random times.

## Pennsylvania Railroad tracks
**Warsaw:** Zimmer Rd.

In December 1882, William Hull's axed and beaten body was found by the railroad tracks. Hull was a big man with gorgeous long black hair, which made him a very striking figure. He owned a butcher shop and was generally liked, but had a penchant for drink and became a bully. John Shaffer, who was accused of fighting him, was charged with murder and convicted. Shaffer appealed and the second trial ended when Hull having was hit by a train. Once the second trial ended in 1883, Hull started his haunting of the railroad. Several people, including railroad engineers, have seen a ghost with an axe and a ghost that flagged down the train.

## Sacred Heart Church and School
**Warsaw:** 135 N. Harrison St.

Visitors to the school gym feel light-headed when entering. In the center of the gym, people feel the hands of many people pushing them. Footprints appear in dust on the floors and a scraping of metal on metal is heard.

## Sawmill Lake
**Leesburg:** Sawmill Rd.

Mists and apparitions are seen. A ghost dubbed "Whitey" by the locals is very noisy. Loud thumps can be heard at random times. A man can be heard yelling. Legend states that a drunk driver crashed into a home over 30 years ago and died.

## Syracuse Creek
**North Webster:** CR N650E south of CR E1120N

In 1903 a small bridge crossed this section of road. A headless woman appeared when people came to cross the bridge. She is still seen today, waiting for the next person to cross the stream.

## Train Tracks
**Winona Lake:** Train tracks east of Winona Lake

Mike Fitzgerald was struck by a passenger train on New Year's Eve 1868. His ghost carries a lantern and continues to walk the tracks. Visitors, investigators, and train men have seen him flagging down the train.

## Tumbleweed Inn
**North Webster:** North Webster

A ghost named Uncle Earl opens and closes the Inn's refrigerator, presumably looking for beer. Another uncle showed up in a WWI uniform to tell his family he was leaving and they wouldn't see him again. The family received a telegram that day saying the uncle had been killed a week earlier. The family also reported the sound of a moving suitcase at night and a mysterious unseen person swinging on the porch swing.

## Warsaw Public Library
**Warsaw** 310 E. Main St.

The building was once used as a checkpoint for the Underground Railroad during pre-Civil War days when slavery was legal. The basement still harbors spirits. Late at night employees have reported hearing children crying and seeing mysterious figures moving about the bookshelves.

# LA GRANGE
# COUNTY

## Brushy Prairie

**Brushy Prairie:** US 20 between CR N1150E and CR N1000W

A Lady in White haunts this road. Her final destination is a cemetery. Similar to Resurrection Mary (seen in Chicago, IL), she wears a beautiful dress and disappears when picked up by motorists.

## Riverside Cemetery

**Lima:** East of SR 9 on CR E500N and 3rd St.

Crissy (aka Christina Hahn; aka Crissy Hand; aka Skunk Girl; aka Skunk Lady; aka Skunk Woman) was born somewhere between 1838 and 1847. The 1870 census has her born in 1847. Her father and mother, Mason and Clarissa Hand died, in a boating accident while she was young, her brother Royal. Her younger sister Henrietta's fate is unknown.

What is known is that she fended for herself. Supposedly marrying four times, Crissy had to fend for herself. was very robust in nature and possibly helped build the railroad tracks around her home. She lived in what most people considered squalor. Animals, mostly skunks, were her friends.

For years, she lived in a house on the northern side of Riverside Cemetery. Later in her life, the people of Howe built her a home on Twin Lake and took care of her. She was a very friendly soul who would converse or share her home with anyone. Although she owned a lot of land, she never sold it and it went to her estate after her death.

She is allegedly buried on the east side of Riverside Cemetery. A plaque commemorates her life. The only person who knew where she was truly buried died before her gravestone was set.

# LA PORTE COUNTY

## 1800 Elston Street
**Michigan City:** 1800 Elston St.

Voices are heard, footsteps, and ghost figures can sometimes be seen. People see a shadowy man in the basement.

## 415 Virginia Avenue
**LaPorte:** 415 Virginia Ave.

The original house was built in 1856 and burnt in 1885. A young teenager died in the fire. In the 1950s the house that was built in the same place was turned into apartments. The people who have died in the area of the apartments still haunt the building. A young woman has been seen warning people of fires. Items in the apartments move on their own. Doors open and close without the aid of human hands.

## County Road 50 North
**Michigan City:** CR 50N off US 421

This area is home to a time warp. The white house that sits at the corner of this location is sometimes not there. At other times, however, people will be able to see it.

## Barker Mansion and Civic Center
**Michigan City:** 631 Washington St.

For years this location has been considered haunted. Built in 1857 by John H. Barker, who built the Haskell & Barker Railroad Car Company, this house embodies gentility.

A handsome apparition of a beautiful young man appears to teenage girls. A woman in Victorian clothing enjoys interacting with tour groups. Visitors and staff see a couple dancing in the home. A small girl bounces a ball down the stairway.

## Belle Gunness House
**LaPorte:** McClung Rd. There are now many houses on the property where the house once stood.

Belle Gunness was a widow with children. People felt sorry for her children, especially when bodies were found in the house. When the search was over, 14 whole people were found with several unclaimed bones and teeth. Apparently Belle had killed her husbands when she tired of them.

In 1908 the Bell Gunness house burned. A burned, decapitated body of a woman was found. The body was possibly Belles, or perhaps one of her victims.

When Belle died, Ray Lamphere was tried and convicted of her death and died of TB in prison. He had been in love with her, and had helped her bury the bodies and he also ground some up for her hogs to eat before slaughter. He also confessed the body in the fire was a homeless woman from Chicago. Belle was supposed to contact him after the incident died down, but she never did.

People hear people screaming, feel cold spots and hear heavy labored breathing as if someone is running.

## Blue Chip Casino
**Michigan City:** 777 Blue Chip Dr.

A woman in a blue sundress and long red hair haunts the casino. She shows herself in guest rooms and in the restroom. The room gets cold. If any water is around, faucets turn on or glasses spill.

## Briar Leaf Golf Course
**LaPorte:** 3233 N Old State Road 39

A spirit likes to pull pranks on visitors. It moves personal items. A member caught the voice of a man saying "Rodney". The former owner was named Rodney Morozowski.

## Fountainview Terrace Nursing & Rehabilitation
**LaPorte:** 1900 Andrew Ave.

The building is rumored to be on top of a Native American burial ground. A female patient was found out of bed, and dead on the floor. She couldn't have gotten out because her bedrails were still up. Today she haunts the buildings.

## Hangman's Road
**LaPorte:** Orr Lake Rd. (the dead end part that goes south)
*(aka Orr Lake Rd.)*

In an old tale of a broken down car, a man goes for help and comes back. He can't find his companion. Seeing a drop of blood on the windshield, he looks and finds her hanging from a tree. Legend states many people have been killed here. People have seen a person hanging in the trees and white figures running through the trees.

## Hesston Steam Museum
LaPorte: 1201 CR E1000N

A ghostly Native American man accompanied by a coal black horse walks by visitors.

## Kingsbury Ordnance Plant
### Kingsford Heights/Kingsbury (near LaPorte): East of US 35 on US 6

*(aka Old Military Base)*

This former ammunitions plant served in WWII and employed over 20,000 people. The plant was a manufacturing facility and housing for workers of the plant. By 1959 the plant had closed and part of the land was sold for the Kingsbury State Fish and Wildlife Area. Visitors see soldiers and civilians walking around the area and report smelling gas. Legend has it that gas explosions occurred during production. Which killed several workers. A hanged man can be seen hanging on a rope, and motioning to visitors.

## LaPorte Cinema
### LaPorte: 608 Colfax Ave.

A young teenage girl haunts the Cinema. She appears in the tile of the floor and appears in the bathroom. She's also been seen in the office and the theater. Her death is unknown; according to legend, she drowned in a nearby pond, fell off a Ferris wheel, or died in a fire in her family's home.

## LaPorte High School
### LaPorte: 602 F St.

A young Native American girl died and her ghost still wanders where she faltered on a small hill across the street from what would become La Porte High School's baseball field. The restrooms in the school flush without reason and the faucets turn themselves on. Cold spots are felt in the school and on the grounds. Lights turn off and on and loud noises are heard when no one is nearby.

## Lambs Chapel Cemetery
### Rolling Prairie: E 600 N and N. Fall Rd.

A beautiful woman runs through the cemetery. She is most frequently seen at night, but she is also seen during the day as well, walking amongst the stones. History states that her car broke down and when she got out to see if she could fix it, a man jumped out and chased her through the cemetery, where he caught and killed her.

## LaPorte Medical Building
### LaPorte:'I' and 10th Streets
*(aka 'I' and 10th Street Clinic, aka the Andrews Mansion)*

Part of the trail of tears, this area was a resting place for the Native Americans as they were pushed west. A young girl died during the winter they stopped at this area. The building is currently a medical clinic. The elevators erratically move from floor to floor and the bathroom doors often lock, trapping occupants. Chairs also skid across the floor, pushed by unseen hands. A woman is also seen in the attic and her footsteps are heard. A woman walks along the back balcony. A man in a suit walks along the porch. The old crank handle doorbell has long been disconnected, but is said to crank on its own. Once, when this happened, there was no one at the door, but footprints were in front of the door (no where else) where someone would have stood. Some believe a little Cherokee girl is haunting the building. Others believe a woman who fell in love with a man who went to the California gold rush is waiting for him to come for her. After he left, she died in a train accident.

## Le Mans Academy
### Rolling Prairie: 5901 N 500 E
*(aka Le Monds Academy)*

The area around Rolling Prairie was settled in 1831 as Nauvoo. It was later called Portland and Plum Grove, because of the wild plum trees. Native Americans were marched through the area on the Trail of Death/Trail of Courage. In 1857 it was named Rolling Prairie. One hundred years later LeMans was established. Although in 2003 the school closed its doors, feelings of uneasiness are sensed here. Investigators have seen orbs, shadow figures and have been touched by unseen hands. Today, the property is owned by the Legionaries of Christ and houses the Sacred Heart Apostolic School.

## Light House Premium Outlet Stores
### Michigan City: 601 Lighthouse Place

Staff and shoppers have had multiple interactions with the ghosts here. A boy looks out the windows. A woman in a long coat walks through the stores.

## Lincoln Elementary School
### LaPorte: 402 Harrison St.

Lights and water turn on and off for no reason.

## Michigan City Prison
### Michigan City 201 Woodlawn Ave.

Shadows and flickering lights are seen within the prison walls. In one cell on cellblock x, an inmate had recently lost his cellmate and he heard someone whisper in his ear, "You're next." The next night, the inmate woke up with someone clawing him. The guards couldn't explain it.

## Old Chicago Road
### Michigan City: Off County Line Rd, on Porter County side.

The Mafia used to use Devil's Bridge as a "family" burial plot. – Apparitions of 1930s era men have been seen. Orbs and mists have been captured on film.

## Old Lighthouse Museum
**Michigan City:** 1 Washington Park Marina

For 150 years, the lighthouse has graced the Lake Michigan coastline. Harriet Colfax, a lighthouse keeper from 1861 to 1904 haunts the museum. Footsteps are heard on the stairs and at times, a translucent figure is seen climbing the stairs. Many people believe it is Ms. Colfax on the stairs.

## Old U.S. 30
**Union Mills:** US 30 between Hanna and CR 600 W

A blue figure has been seen at the railroad for over 20 years. In 1987 a man was hit by a train at 3 am. Today around the same time, he can be seen carrying a lantern.

## Orr Lake Road
**LaPorte:** N.Orr Lake Rd south of W 150 N

A doctor's wife and daughter died. He was so distraught he preserved them in pickle brine. Today the doctor is long dead but you can see him and his servant (the Hookman) reenact the pickling every full moon in the woods.

*(See also Hangman's Road)*

## Patton Cemetery
**LaPorte:** North of SR 4 entrance off Clement St.
*(aka Patten Cemetery)*

Belle Gunness is buried in this cemetery. She and others are said to walk through the cemetery as if they don't know they are dead.

*(See Belle Gunness House, LaPorte, LaPorte Co.)*

## Posey Chapel Cemetery
**LaPorte:** Corner of E1000N and N400E

A preacher hung himself from a tree next to the gate. Visitors see the residual haunting of this event. Orbs, EVPs and moans have been captured. One EVP features a woman singing and a guitar playing. A transparent nun is said to cross the street at this location and disappear. Also, a white mist is seen at the top of the hill.

## Range Road Pond
**LaPorte:** Range Rd. and E 700 N

On March 26, 1993 Rayna Rison went missing. A month later her body was found in this pond. Many visitors report feeling a heaviness, even without knowing the unfortunate story. Several visitors report seeing a swirling mist around the pond, and hearing footsteps.

## Saugany Lake
**LaPorte:** Saugana Trail and N 600 E

Chief Suagany protects this lake from any negative energy and events.

## Soldiers Memorial Park
**LaPorte:** Grangemouth and Waverly Rds.

In 1930 a small boy drowned in Stone Lake near the bridge. He haunts the walking trails and can be seen walking down them or near the bridge. When people have tried to talk to him, he laughs and disappears. Sometimes, he will say "hello" or tell "he can't stay" and walks back to the woods.

# LAKE
# COUNTY

## 173 Avenue and Holtz Road

**Lowell:** Intersection 173 Ave. and Holtz Rd.

Driving east on 173rd St, at the top of the first hill, you can see Holtz Rd. Many people have reported seeing accident scene lights on the second hill. When getting to the second hill, the lights and vehicles are gone.

## 36 Detroit Street

**Hammond:** 36 Detroit St.

In this home and on the entire block, strange occurrences happen. Visitors and residents feel cold spots, feel icy unseen hands touch them and witness levitating items. Several visitors have had books, magazines and a vase thrown at them. Many residents say that someone unseen watches in many of the homes.

## 501 Indiana Street

**Hobart:** 501 Indiana St.

The Spencer family was well-to- do. The oldest child killed his sister, Mary and while in jail, he committed suicide. The murder is reenacted in the home. Investigators have heard a child running through the house and have heard piercing screams.

## Bishop Noll Institute

**Hammond:** 1519 E. Hoffman St.

This organization has many spirits. In A-Wing's second floor, visitors, staff and students hear footsteps and talking. In the classrooms, chairs tip over without provocation. Several deaths have occurred on site including one in front of the library, and the now unused pool, and in A-Wing on the second floor where a janitor hung himself. Additionally a girl who was turned down for a part in a play killed herself in the auditorium. Now, anyone who auditions for the lead gets hurt, has mishaps or becomes ill. The library has permanent cold spots and visitors to the empty pool area hear laughter at all hours of the day- and night.

## Black Oak Neighborhood

**Gary:** The Black Oak Neighborhood is located in the SW part of Gary. It is bounded by (roughly) Cline Ave., US80, Chase St., and W. Ridge Rd. Exact location of the school is unknown.

An old schoolhouse which was once a speakeasy and home to prostitution now houses many leftover spirits. Visitors used to hear voices of men going into the basement. A woman in red walks inside the building and outside on the grounds. Often she is crying. Even though the school house has been razed, people still experience the phenomenon associated with this location.

## Circus Train accident

**Ivanhoe (near Hammond):** Ivanhoe is east of Cline St. on W 9th Ave. near Hammond. The tracks that the circus train took run north from W. 9th St. and curve east and go past Kennedy Ave.

On June 23, 1918, the Hagenbeck Wallis circus train crashed and killed over 100 people and animals. Locals believe that it is the animals, and not the people who haunt the nearby woods, although some investigators have picked up EVPs of human voices.

*(Note: Most of the people who died are buried in Woodlawn Cemetery (Forest Park, Illinois) in the area known as Showman's Rest)*

## Cline Avenue

**East Chicago:** Cline Ave. between East Chicago and Griffith, Indiana

Sophia, a Polish immigrant fell in love with someone who wasn't Polish. They decided to get married secretly; she waited in the church. He never showed. Distraught, she threw herself into the Calumet River. She still walks along Cline Ave and the river.

## Crown Point High School

**Crown Point:** 1500 S. Main St.

The school was built on a cemetery. Unearthed several graves in order to build the school. The site was once Luther's Grove, which was owned by an early Crown Point family with same name. Lights throughout the building turn off and on, especially in the gymnasium. Sports equipment moves by unseen hands. Voices are heard in different classrooms and to stop when doors open. The auditorium catwalk is haunted by spirits who are seen walking high above the stage.

## East Chicago Marina

**East Chicago:** 3301 Aldis St.

A handsome gentleman ghost assists visitors. One woman had a conversation with him. He told her he normally doesn't show himself but she reminded him of his daughter. Then he disappeared.

## East Chicago Public Library

**East Chicago:** 2401 E Columbus Dr.

Patrons hear voices. Staff see books removed from shelves when no one is present.

## Fairchild House
**DeMotte:** 212 Ninth St. SW

Orbs were captured on film and whispers are heard throughout the house.

## Forrest Hill Neighborhood
**Merrillville:** One block east of Broadway St.
The Potawatomi lived here. Animals react to unseen things by barking, growling, hissing and running

## Gavit High School
**Hammond:** 1670 175th St.

People report hearing footsteps on the roof as well as seeing a ghost who likes to open windows. Students hear screams at odd hours at evening events. White figures walk the halls.

## Grand Boulevard Lake
**Lake Station:** West side of Grand Boulevard Lake

A man is seen as a residual haunting and a gun shot is heard. Interestingly enough, Andy Figueroa was found dead here one June morning inside his car.

## Grand Kankakee Marsh
**Lowell:** 21690 Clay St.

Although the house that used to sit on this property is long gone, the whole area is believed to have been part of a Native American burial ground. Visitors and investigators report seeing Native American figures, and capturing orbs on pictures. Strange mists are seen throughout the property. A female Native American walks the property and seems very "thoughtful".

## Griffith High School
**Griffith:** 600 N. Wiggs St.

A girl appears in the mirrors in the bathroom next to the auditorium. The legend states that a girl hung herself in the bathroom with an oversized belt. In the school library, chairs tip over and books fly from shelves. The occurrences are believed to be from a ghost of a young man who died of a heart attack in the library.
cars, gives directions to her home and disappears at the cemetery—usually with the driver's jacket on. Drivers who venture into the cemetery find their jackets on her tombstone.

## Hedgewisch Baptist Church of Highland
**Highland:** 8711 Cottage Grove Rd.

This church is said to use exorcism rituals on a regular basis. In 1992, Pastor Win Worley held an open house for anyone needing an exorcism. Over 500 people from a number of states and countries attended. Today, some of the exorcised spirits are said to haunt this church.

## Highland High School
**Highland:** 9135 Erie St.

Bobby Haymaker walks through the hall and does laps in the gym. Basketballs also bounce by unseen hands in the gym. Bobby died during gym class.

## Hobart Cemetery
**Hobart:** At Front St. and E. Cleveland Ave.
*(aka Crybaby Woods)*

A baby cries in the cemetery. Visitors have photographed orbs and mists.

## Indiana Bridge
**Lowell:** Two miles east of I65 on Clay St.

Three people were murdered and thrown off the bridge here. Their spirits are seen falling from the bridge. Mysterious fogs are also reported in the area.

## The John Dillinger Museum
**Hammond:** 7770 Corine Dr.

John Dillinger was a notorious gangster/bank robber in the early 1930s. Aside from a few minor crimes, he was thrown in jail, after a bank robbery. In 1933 he was paroled and then went on the robbing sprees he is most famous for. His short-lived reign as a wanted man came to an end on July 22, 1934 at the Biograph Theater in Chicago when he was gunned down in an FBI trap.

Dillinger is said to haunt many places in Indiana- the location of his boyhood home, Crown Hill Cemetery, where he is buried, the Slippery Noodle in Indianapolis. He also haunts this museum.

Visitors and staff hear his voice (and possibly the voices of his gang) in a possible residual energy type interaction. Additionally, he speaks to visitors. One notable incident involved a small child. An unseen person informed his mother that the boy put something in his mouth. The mother checked and he had indeed put money in his mouth. The boy later said, pointing to a photo of Dillinger, that he tried to take money from the boy.

## Kahler School
**Dyer:** 600 Joliet St.
*Cemetery is St Joseph Cemetery to the east of the school.*

Agnes Kahler haunts the school because she couldn't stop teaching even after 50 years! Books fly from library shelves and toilets flush when no one is around. One student reports going down a hallway in which several lockers opened, slamming the doors back on their hinges. In Agnes Kahler's classroom, boards fall from walls and the door swings open. Additionally, the door has been seen opening and closing as if someone is entering or exiting. Maps hanging on the wall unroll in the room. Alarms go off without reason on a regular basis Kahler is buried at the cemetery next door. Even the assistant principal, Tim Doyle, has a story. A few years ago, the motion detector on the exit nearest the cemetery was tripped. On the surveillance video, a grey blur was seen exiting toward the cemetery. When the old part of the school was torn down, a memorial plaque for Miss Kahler disappeared out of a locked classroom when it had been taken down for cleaning. A boarded up window fell out of its frame.

## Kaske Home Historical Museum
**Munster:** 1005 Ridge Rd.
*(aka Munster Historical Society, Stallbohm-Kaske House Historical Museum; Bieker House)*

Built as a private home in 1837, legend has it that the original home burnt down on Halloween 1949. Now it is a historical society. The attached barn was (which was destroyed by arson) haunted by dark shifting shadows and a figure of Wilhelmina Kaske (Shallbohm) who would lean out the window and sometimes wave. The upstairs of the historical society is haunted by a figure that once threw a can of open paint at a painter. Visitors and staff feel cold spots throughout the building, most notably in the upstairs rooms, and hear footsteps. A child runs around the home and you can hear its footsteps and giggles. A piano plays with no one around. Faces appear in pictures.

The Kaske home is part of Heritage park and rumors abound that the Kaske family was buried in the park. Indeed in the twilight hours and late into the evening, misty figures roam the grounds.

## La Llorna
### Hammond: Between Cline and 5th Avenues

A female ghost in a white blood-stained dress roams the area. This story is told in many cultures. In Indiana, she is said to have had children outside marriage. Because the father wouldn't marry her, she killed them all. When she told him what she'd done, he threw her out. She felt very bad and searched for the kids. When the police finally found out, she'd either killed herself or been killed by or at the river. Today, people still see her searching and crying.

## Lake County Historical Museum
### Crown Point: Old Lake Courthouse, Courthouse Square, Suite 202

A seal impresser was missing for months and later found on a windowsill. When they picked it up, dust was under as though the seal had just been placed in the location. They believe it is Avis Brown, a previous historian playing a prank.

## Lake Prairie Cemetery

**Lowell:** Wicker Blvd. and W. 181st Ave.

Investigators have captured orbs and mists on film. Many of the investigators believe that the mists are the same spirits as the apparitions seen in the cemetery.

## Lillian Holly House

**Crown Point:** 205 E. South St.

This Queen Anne home was built in 1890 for Flora Norta Biggs (widow of James H Biggs). Lillian Holley lived in this home probably longer than anyone and died in it at the age of 102 in 1994. Today, she's seen rocking on the front porch.

## Little Red Schoolhouse

**Hammond:** 7205 Kennedy Ave.

Colored lights dart about the place. A small ghost boy hangs out in the school and walks along the road with his books.

## Lowell Police Department

**Lowell:** 428 E. Commercial Ave.

Jail keys are heard in locks and on chains. Staff heard footsteps going upstairs. It is now occupied by the Chamber of Commerce.

## Lowell Public Library

**Lowell:** 1505 E. Commercial Ave.

Flanked by Lowell Memorial Cemetery on one side, and a tombstone manufacturer on the other, it is no wonder this library has paranormal issues. Employees, both current and former, have noticed doors opening and closing by themselves, music playing from an empty storage room, books falling in succession from different parts of the building, and interesting odors.

## Michael Jackson's Boyhood Home

**Gary:** 2300 Jackson St.

Michael Jackson, 80s iconic popstar, surprises visitors by appearing to them. Orbs of light also permeate the property. The cries of children scare visitors. Some people believe all of this is residual energy from when the Jackson family lived in the home.

## Old Botanical Gardens
**Hammond:** 626 177th St.

*(aka Reaper's Realm; aka Jayme House)*

Joseph E. Meyer founded a packager herb company in 1910 and constructed the Botanical Gardens building in 1926. At one point the second floor was damaged by fire.

The former owners died and now haunt the location. People hear walking upstairs when they are alone. In the woods behind the gardens, white, misty figures walk through the trees. When Reaper's Realm takes place, two women are reported as helping, although they are unknown to the people on site. Lights turn on even though the batteries aren't in the lights. Automated mannequins for the haunted house functioned, although their power source wasn't active. One ghost, referred to as Mary is blamed for many of the incidents. One woman is heard crying in an upper floor.

The bedrooms are haunted. The one to the left of the stairs on the second floor has a small closet- the door is often found open. In the bedroom to the right, smells, noises and glowing eyes are reported. Children laughing and playing surprise visitors.

*(Note: Some folks believe this location is also the site of the Jayme House, which is attributed to being an old saloon, although no proof of this history is evident.)*

## Old Homestead
**Crown Point:** 227 S. Court St.

The oldest home Lake County was built in 1847 by Wellington A Clark. Visitors hear children playing in the home as well as footsteps when no one is around. Items go missing in the home, which is in the process of restoration.

## Old Lake County Jail
**Crown Point:** 232 S. Main St.

This jail's claim to fame is John Dillinger's escape from it using a soap gun. In use until 1960, visitors see mists and orbs as well as hear footsteps. Jail doors slam and staff and visitors hear harsh words from men. Investigators saw a transparent woman on the main stairs. Sounds of stones skipping across the floor are often heard- which was a way that inmates communicated. One investigation team caught an EVP that said, "Shut that damn thing off." A man answering as Everett Daniels, US Army, also identified himself. Later it was discovered his family donated items to the museum. Visitors feel fingers in their hair and touches on their arms and legs. Many visitors have had "things" brush past them. Orbs are captured in pictures. Screams come from the catacomb area. Shadow figures are seen walking through the entire structure and even a typewriter has functioned on its own.

## Phantom of the Open Hearth at U.S. Steel
**Gary:** One North Broadway

A worker who fell into a vat of hot steel appears when the steel is poured.

## Reder Road
**Griffith:** S. Colfax St to Reder Rd (Ct.). Reder Road has been partially closed down and is quite overgrown. The railroad tracks are still accessible.
*(aka Reeder Road; see Ross Cemetery, Griffith, Lake Co.)*

This location has many stories. Elizabeth Wilson drowned in a nearby swamp in a car accident. She haunts the side of the road waiting for a ride home. When you reach Ross Cemetery she disappears. Many people speculate this disappearance is because she was buried in Ross Cemetery.

Also associated with this location is the classic boyfriend hanging above the car story. A boy and girl are cuddling and hear a scraping sound outside the car. He goes to investigate. After a while the girl still hears scraping and is worried that her boyfriend hasn't returned. When she gets out, he's hanging from a tree by his neck/feet with a belt, a rope, etc. and his class ring and/or feet are scraping on the top of the car.

The solstices and equinoxes are equally busy times for the area. Some people claim satanic rituals occur in the cemetery and nearby fields. Additionally, a path that leads down the road is said to take you to a church. There you can hear the screams of a parishoner driven to insanity and death by a mentally disturbed pastor. On your way there, you pass railroad tracks that host a dark shadow man who will follow you down the tracks and down the path.

This area has long been associated with mafia connections, not only from the bodies found in the area but also the bootleg and other business deals made in the area in serene privacy.

## Ridge Road
**Gary:** Ridge Rd., most often seen between Kennedy Ave and Broadway.

A woman in a wedding gown walks this road. She killed herself in Calumet River on Halloween night.

## River Forrest Jr. Sr High Schools
**Hobart:** 3300 Indiana St.

These two schools were at one time separate. The tennis courts used to house the pool for PE. A child drowned at the school, so they demolished the pool. The boy is seen in the high school gym, and in the jr school multipurpose rooms and the high school cafeteria.

He only comes out at night, especially for school sponsored events. Not seen during school hours- late night for events. Janitors don't like being in the school after 9pm because of all the noise- including chairs and desks moving.

## Ross Cemetery

**Griffith:** Whitcomb St and W. 50th Ave.

Elizabeth Wilson died in a car accident off of Reeder Rd (see entry) and is buried in the cemetery. Her boyfriend was pinned in the car. She gets into

## Sacred Heart Elementary

**Whiting:** 1731 Laporte Ave

Closed in 1999 due to financial issues, this school hosted several priests and nuns who came to the area to retire. Chairs are pushed and moved throughout the school. Teacher and students voices scared the janitorial staff and early arrivers at the school.

## Saint Casimir's School

**Hammond:** 4329 Cameron Ave.

*(aka Resurrection)*

A janitor and a girl who died in the 1953 fire haunt the school. The girl roams the halls near the restrooms. The janitor is often seen at the opposite end of the hallway. He will look at you, then moves his mop bucket down the hallway or into a classroom and disappears.

## Sherwood Lake Apartments

**Schererville:** 801 E. Sherwood Lake Dr.

A woman pushed her son in the lake while they were feeding ducks because she got mad at him. Her son drowned. The boy is seen in the pond and people have heard his screams.

## Southeast Grove Cemetery

**Crown Point:** From 153rd Ave. turn right onto Southgrove Rd. Look for entrance on left (if you get to 157th Ave, you've missed the turn off.)

*(aka Gypsy Graveyard)*

Glowing figures, mists and orbs are seen at the cemetery. The ghosts are attributed to the many gypsies who were sick and died on the spot. Behind the cemetery, the ghost of a wolf/dog chases visitors but never quite catches them.

## Whihala Beach

**Whiting:** In Whihala Beach County Park (near Lake Shore Dr. on Lake Michigan)

In the woods by the beach, visitors see ghostly outlines of sailboats and bathers. Laughter and water splashing is also heard.

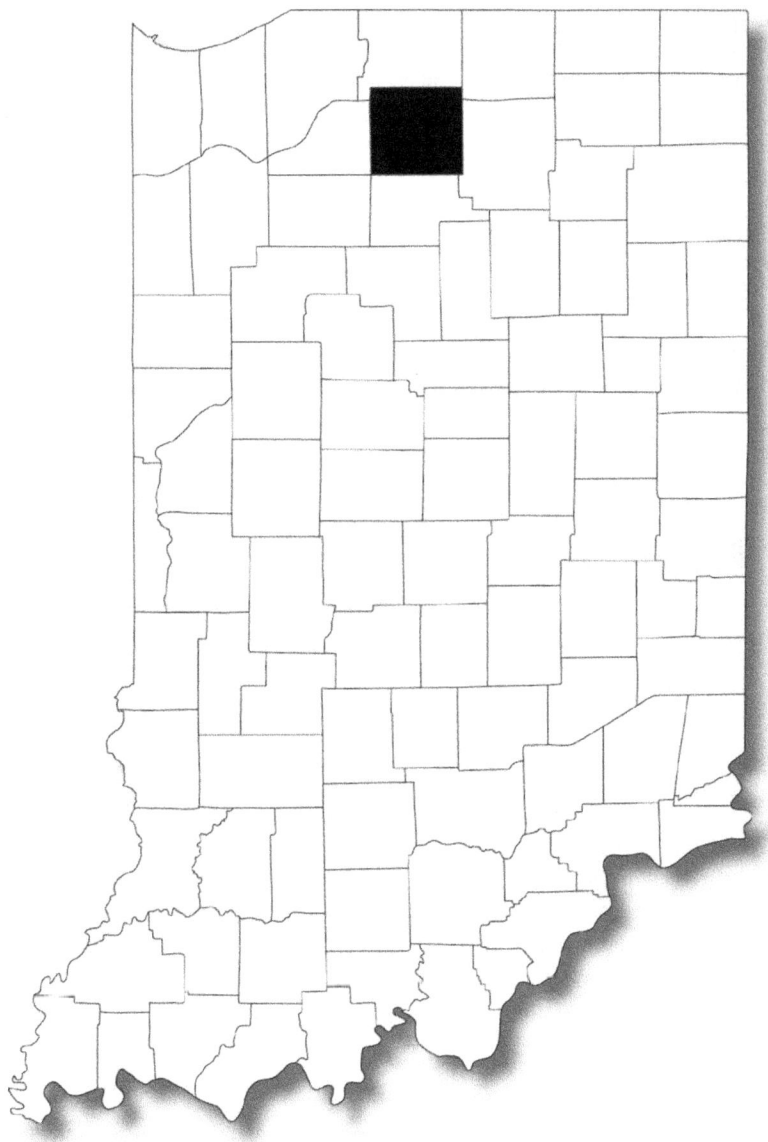

# MARSHALL COUNTY

## 118 South Center Street
**Plymouth:** 118 S. Center St.

This house is over 100 years old. Various tenants have reported cabinets opening, cold chills and lights turning off and on. One person was shoved and reportedly had a slight head injury. Apparitions that interact with residents are seen on stairs. One room in particular seems to have quite a bit of activity. Tenants tell of blankets being flung off them, and of having their faces pushed down in pillows.

## 8th Road Haunted House
**Bourbon:** 8th Rd.

The daughter and wife of a farmer were raped and killed, their bodies thrown in the woods. The husband and son were hung in the barn. At midnight you see the ropes in the barn, and you see the wife and daughter running toward the woods and hear their screams.

## Ancilla College and Convent
**Donaldson:** 9601 S. Union Rd.

Nuns walk the tunnels of the convent and college disappearing into walls or before your eyes. Visitors have been pinched, pushed and scratched in the tunnels. Doors and windows open and close on their own. Items move around the kitchen at will.

## Ewald Cemetery
**Bremen:** 5th Rd. east of Hawthorn
*(aka Little Egypt Cemetery)*

Apparitions are seen in the cemetery. Handprints appear on your car. If you walk by a baby's tombstone you hear it cry. A phantom farmer will chase you out of the cemetery- he died in a field nearby. Headlights follow you through the cemetery. In the woods down the street, a teenage girl was raped and killed. You hear her screams in the woods.

## The Granary
**Inwood:** Next to the old post office

An old farmer in white overalls haunts the town granary. He tells you to leave because he is protecting the area. One person who visited the area in the early morning saw him standing on top the granary and watched him fall, but never hit the ground. Others have seen him in the window of the office. He has a black/white striped hat and just stares at you.

## Hayloft Restaurant
**Plymouth:** SR30 and SR31
*(Note: The restaurant burned to the ground and is being rebuilt.)*

The Hayloft was originally a barn from the 1800s, in the 1970s this building was turned into a restaurant. The spirits here move items in the restaurant- glasses, table cloths, tables, and pots and pans. One of the spirits appears as a farmer preceded by the smell of burning wood. People have named the ghost of a farmer, Homer. He spends a lot of time in the Silo Room and in the kitchen. He's seen from about the waist or knees up. The staff blame Homer for items disappearing altogether or for making noises by dropping things. Patrons report a Native American who stands in various parts of the restaurant. He's blamed for displacing chairs and banging the pots and pans in the kitchen. Since this building has burnt down, some investigators speculate the ghosts were warning the owners about the fire.

## Muckshaw Road
**Plymouth:** Muckshaw Rd.

An old truck full of ghost teenagers is seen. The teens died in an accident. On full moons, the truck will chase you.

## Nighthart Cemetery
**Plymouth:** 7th Rd. near Jarrah Rd.

A seven foot tall shadow figure swoops around the cemetery. A loud, high pitched cry is heard.

## Old Fire Station
**Oaklandon:** Northeast corner of Broadway St. and Oaklandon Rd.

Myterious shadows wind through the building and the bay doors open and close at random times.

## State Road 117 and State Road 110
**Plymouth:** SR117 and SR110

Paukooshuck, son of Potawatomi Chief Aubbeenaubbee is said to walk the road. He spent his life in the area. Paukooshuck walked the Trail of Tears although he was unsuccessful. Eventually he entered Chief Winamac's village and died after being in a fight.

## Troll Bridge
**Bremen:** On 5th Rd., between Filbert Trail and N Grape Rd.
*Near Little Egypt (see entry for Little Egypt)*

The area is very quiet and when the paranormal happens, it is as silent as the grave. Strange lights are seen around the bridge and in the trees. A snake that transforms into a wolf is seen uncoiling from the trees to the right of the bridge. A tall dark shadow figure chases you. Investigators have reported batteries draining immediately and even fresh batteries from a brand new, never opened, package have gone dead. Once they've left the cemetery, the batteries remain dead. No sign of a troll, though!

## Uptown Cinema

**Culver:** 612 E. Lake Shore Dr.

*(aka Uptown Theater)*

In the 1920s Culver had several theaters on its main streets. Vaudeville was on the bill at Uptown as well as movies. The theater was changed to El Rancho in the 1930s as it looked like a fort. It has gone through many ups and downs, and the current owner is hard at work making this landmark a viable entertainments spot in Culver. Spirits of former patrons and performers are seen still moving about the theater.

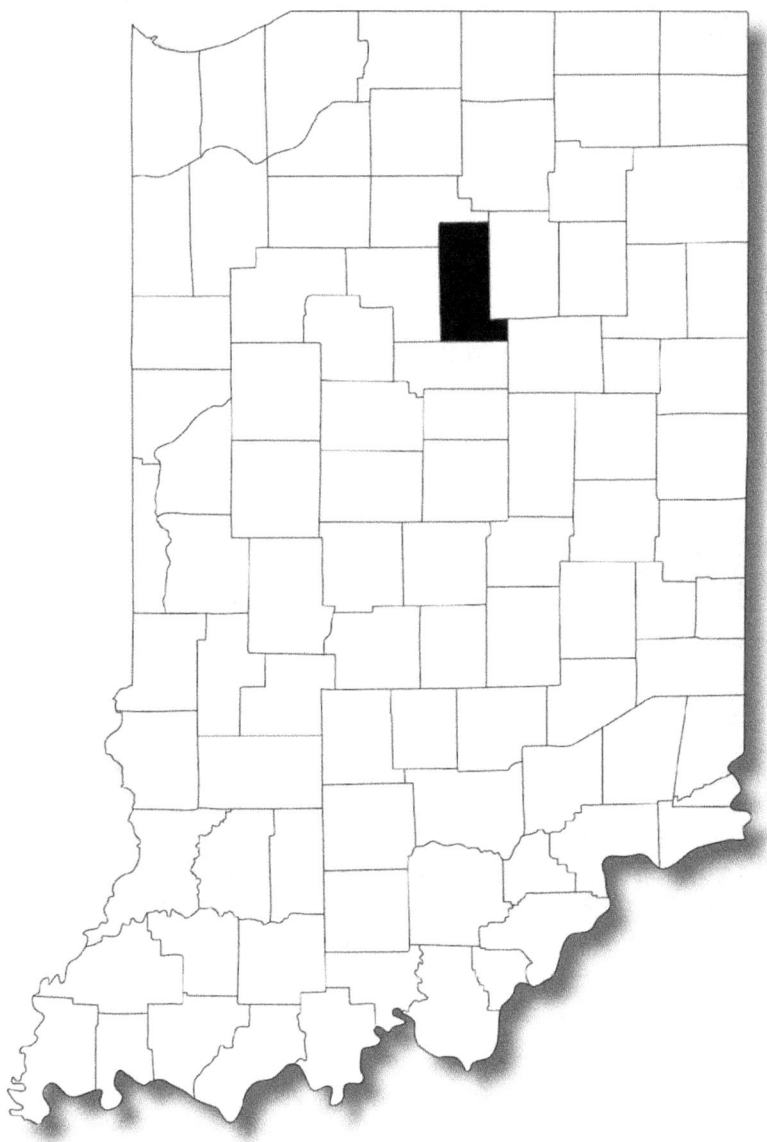

# MIAMI
# COUNTY

## 101 W. Ottawa Street
**Miami:** 101 W. Ottawa St.

During a renovation this home began to experience ghostly activity. Pictures fly off walls and hit the occupants. Items are flung off tables though no one touches them. A helpful spirit unplugs electric appliances that are left on. Perfumed air wafts frequently through the location. Animals react to unseen spirits by making noise, running away, and cowering. People are jerked by unseen hands that don't want to let go.

## 63 W. 6th Street
**Peru:** 63 W 6th St.

A ghost woman opens the upstairs curtains and moves things kept in storage there. Sometimes she is heard walking down the stairs.

## Converse *(see Grant County)*

## Five Corners Cemetery
**Macy:** On W 12150 N east of Old US 31

Unexplained lights and apparitions are reported. Moving orbs have been captured on film

## Grissom Air Force Base
*(aka Bunker Hill)*
**Peru:** 1000 W. Hoosier Blvd.

In 1968 a B-58 Hustler pilot was killed as the landing gear collapsed. Once the fire that killed the pilot was out and the plane was safe to move, a man named Tom wanted to make sure that the fire was indeed out and no smoldering remained. As he stood near the aircraft, he noticed new footprints going from the aircraft to where it would have been a safe spot for the pilot, had he had a chance. The only other prints were his own. Following the other prints, he noticed they became lighter and lighter and disappeared.

## Leonda Cemetery
**Peru:** 1539 W 600 S (no public access)
*(aka Kings Court; aka Kings Court Mobile Home Park)*

Cemetery behind the park is haunted by woodland fairies and pixies.

## Mississinawa Battle Grounds
**Peru:** 7 miles north of Marion. Take I-69 to SR 18 East. In Marion, follow SR 15 north, following the signs to Mississinawa 1812.

Battles are still reenacted by invisible people. Guns and cries for help are heard. Many apparitions of men, women and children walk the lake. The caves around the area also contain shadow people.

## Okie Pinokie

**Peru:** Take IN 124 east from Peru. Turn right onto 150 S (Fire Lane). Drive for a couple of miles until you come to a roundabout.

Native Americans have been seen running through the woods. Some appear to be residual hauntings, yet others have interacted with visitors. One visitor reports having had a Native American guide help him find his way out of the wooded area and back to the road. Other people report similar experiences, although some believe the area is a time and space warp. EVPs of voices have been heard, some seemingly in a language other than English. Some people believe there are hundreds of spirits in the woods at this location.

## Old Miami County Jail

**Peru:** 5th and Wabash Streets

Now used as a haunted house at Halloween, some of the volunteers and visitors to the haunted house say the made up ghosts aren't the only kind in this former jail. Apparitions of men in work clothes and a woman in a 1940s pencil skirt and blouse have been witnessed.

## Old Stone House

**Peru:** 2372 Old Stone Rd.

Now Christian Life Fellowship Church, this home was part of the Underground Railroad. Lights emanate from the home and shadow figures with lanterns are seen running to and from the river. The oldest part of the building burned and was remodeled on the inside.

## Peaceful Acres Mobile Home Court

**Peru:** Lot 3 Peaceful Acres, 5485 Road 31 South

An apparition of a man (sometimes called "the Toothless Wonder") haunts Lot 3 of Peaceful Acres Mobile Home Park.

## St. John's Lutheran Cemetery/St. Charles Catholic Cemetery

**Peru:** End of N Kelly Ave. Only the Lutheran cemetery has a sign.

A stairway appears descending from the white cross in St. Charles Catholic Cemetery.

## Seven Pillars
**Peru:** On old Francis Slocum Trail; 3 miles east of Peru

Used by the Miami Native Americans, its Tribal Council met here to converse with their elders. It was also a trading post. French believed that the spirits of the dead were all around them and had special items to keep them at bay. It used to be a camping and fishing site. Ghosts have been seen walking through the area, in the water. The area has been repurchased by the Miami as part of their efforts to be reestablished as a recognized tribe.

## Tillet Cemetery
*(aka Tillett's Cemetery; aka Hook man's Cemetery)*

**Peru:** At the crossroads of US 24 and E. Lovers Lane. Go east of US 24 onto the first dirt road to your left. Cemetery is in wooded area.

A mist is always present and always quiet. A cold area surrounds the Hook man's grave. Sometimes he is seen on the lane walking toward parked cars. Photos of blurred apparitions have been captured as well as photos with shadow people.

## Wabash River by Jacob Rife's gravel pit
**Peru:** Wabash River by Jacob Rife's gravel pit. It's across from West City Park (a house sits on the site).

A skeleton was found in the dirt as they excavated in 1927. Jacob Rife's bones were given the to the Miami Historical society. Since then, screams have been heard, mists have been prevalent and pleas for help are heard.

# NEWTON
# COUNTY

## Body Cemetery
**Kentland:** 1 mile west of Woodland on E. 1400 North Rd.

(Pronounced BO-dee.) Alfonso's grave glows- it is the only grave you can see as you approach the cemetery. Legend has it that the cemetery was once home to a Native American burial site. It is an interesting cemetery, as it is a sand dune.

## Cast Park
**Kentland:** N. First St. and Old US41

Named for Alvin C. Cast, who was a well respected member of the community, and served as an educator, leader and businessman. The walking paths have been home to shadow figures running between trees. The sound of someone out of breath as if from running is heard and occasionally, a bright green light is seen on the walking paths although no source is ever found.

## Kentland Community Center
**Kentland:** Corner of Fourth and Lincoln Streets

A figure of an old man is seen around the pool. A woman in white walks through the building after dark lighting each room she passes through.

## Lantern Lane
**Kentland:** 1980E and W1200N in Woodland, IL. A mailbox in a cement post marks the lane's location.

A floating lantern greets visitors. Sometimes, it glows a soft white-yellow; other times it is a white hot blue color. One legend centers on a woman who was waiting for her husband to return. When he didn't return after night fall, she went to find him. Neither was heard from again. Some people believe the lantern is held by the woman looking for her husband. When the house they lived in still existed, a visitor decided to take something from the home and it turned hot, burning her hands.

Another legend is that a glut of horse thieves in the area were hung from trees at Lantern Lane and you can see their ghosts on many nights. Some visitors have indicated that when the blue light appears, they can see people hanging from the trees.

## Old Gas Station House
**Lake Village:** Unknown

People hear pounding on the walls throughout the building. Spectral people roam the rooms, emitting bright flashes of light.

# NOBLE
# COUNTY

## Albion Jail Museum

**Albion:** 215 W. Main St.

*(aka Noble County Old Jail Museum)*

Visitors have felt hands on shoulders, taps on arms and cold breezes.

## East Noble High School

**Kendallville:** 901 Garden St.

A man is seen in the gymnasium in the bleachers and walking next to people. A girl who died in the science room in the 1980s likes to trick janitors by turning the television on.

## Ligonier Public Library

**Ligonier:** 300 South Main St.

Reports of temperature drops, high EMF readings, and orbs. Staff members have had experiences of the ghost, from sightings to the sounds of footsteps. Books have even flown of the shelves and objects have been moved.

## Restoration Lutheran Church

**Kendallville:** 500 E. Mitchell St.

Unseen footsteps are heard walking up and down stairs. Mirrors show faces from other people and times. Temperature spikes and drops occur. Shadow figures move furniture and sometimes chase you. One person is said to have had scratch marks down her back. The kitchen in the basement has a lot of activity. A dark figure slowly appears and makes you feel very uncomfortable.

## Spook Hill

**Kendallville:** 9663 E 1000 N

A pack-peddler, or traveling peddler who carried his wares in a pack, was murdered by the property owner in the barn over 130 years ago. A mysterious shape could be seen moving from the house to the barn every night after the murder.

## Strand Theater

**Kendallville:** 221 S. Main St.

Built as an opera house in the 1800s, it is now haunted by ghosts of the past. In the balcony and projection areas, a man stands and watches whoever is in the theater. He's been seen for several decades. One owner doesn't believe that the activity is related to ghosts, but could possibly be a source of negative energy.

# PORTER
# COUNTY

## Bailey Homestead
**Chesterton:** Mineral Springs Rd. between US 20 and US 12

The house was built by Honore Gratien Joseph Bailly de Messein who helped settle the Calumet region of Indiana. His trading post was known far and wide as a fair place for both white and Native American people. Ghost children play with the children who visit. A young man walks through the property during the day. He wears a white shirt and rough sewn breeches.

## Baum Bridge Road Inn
**Kouts:** 1092 South Baums Bridge Rd.

Once a stop for people traveling through the Kankankee River Valley, this paranormal hotspot includes orb sightings and EVP activity. A man with an aura light around him is seen in the Inn. When you look for him, he will automatically appear in front of you.

## Brown Mansion
**Chesterton:** 700 W. Porter Ave.
*(aka Westchester Township History Museum)*

In 1885, George Brown built this home for his family. Very prominent in the community, he married Charity Carter in 1855.

A short year after they moved in to the Brown Mansion, George Sr. and George Jr. were very ill. George Sr.'s son James contracted typhoid in 1888. In 1889 his son Charles died at 18 of complications of typhoid fever contracted at age two. Charity had cancer in 1894 and was confined to a wheelchair until her death in 1895. Daughter Anna, who was married in the home, was divorced less than 8 years later. In 1899, George died. A year later the house burned but was salvageable.

The mansion was once turned into apartments, and the ballroom used as storage for the museum. Eventually the house was sold to Dr. Gustafson from Indianapolis who rented it out. In the 1950s, Bill and Jeanne Gland rented the home talking about their ghost "Ebbie".

## Camp Lawrence
**Valparaiso:** 68 E. 700 N.

Legend states that in the 1970s the maintenance director Joseph John O'Connell was killed. Witnesses claim it was a creature such as a yeti. This creature has been seen around the area since.

## Campbell Street
**Valparaiso:** Campbell St.

Annabel went against her parent's wishes. They wanted her to be a schoolteacher in the area. She met a man and went courting, and got married. As soon as she had a baby boy, she quit teaching. Her husband drank a lot and money stress didn't help. She escaped with her child, making her way over the fields in the cold night. She died in the snow. Now people see her in the trees next to the road asking for help. Sometimes you can hear her yelling "Help me," and walking as a white figure.

## Chellberg Farm
**Chesterton:** Mineral Springs Rd. between US 20 and US 12

This 1885 homestead is now a museum. It was built by Anders and Johanna Chellberg, who were part of the Swedish community. A ghost woman, who is very particular about the house, tends to tell people to wipe their feet and be tidy while in the house.

## Court Restaurant
**Valparaiso:** 69 Franklin St.

Built in 1885 as an undertaking establishment, it changed to a furniture store, funeral home, a barber shop, an American Legion hall and finally a restaurant. The names have changed over the years, Royallee Restaurant and Lounge, This Side Up, Court Restaurant and 69 East. But the people haven't changed. Cold drafts are felt (especially in the men's restaurant), lights turn on and off as well. Footsteps are heard and orbs have been captured on film. The scent of roses and tobacco are also experienced. A woman named Marsha says hello to visitors.

## Crisman School
**Portage:** 6161 Old Porter Rd.

The school is haunted by several apparitions of teachers who have passed away.

## Dewey House
**Valparaiso:** The Dewey House is no longer standing. It burned to the ground in 2000. Today, what people believe is the Dewey House (at the curve of 650 N and 125 W) is actually a private residence (it's now been razed and there is a newer home in its place). The Dewey location is to the west of this on the north side of 650 N.

*(aka Dewey's House; aka Old Man Dewey's House)*

One of the most widespread legends in the Valpo area, the story goes that in 1954 Mr. Dewey lost his job because of alcohol. He killed his family and chopped their heads off, staking them on the gate posts near the road. He then hung himself in a grain silo. Today, many people believe you can still see blood on the walls and the hounds of hell guard the gates to the house. Other people report seeing red eyes and orbs in the woods.

Part of the legend occurs after Mr. Dewey died. Someone bought the house and started to remodel. One of the workers fell through the floor and landed on a pitchfork. Although there is no concrete evidence of this story, there was a similar murder in another state in April 1955 in which a Mr. Duncan died in prison before his trial. Mr. Dewey Babcock (his real name), died in 1986 in Whispering Pines Nursing home. His wife died after him.

## Diana Of The Dunes
### Chesterton/Porter: 1600 N. 25E
*(aka Ogden Dunes)*

Once uninhabited, what is now the Dunes State Park was open dunes. Fishermen and locals would occasionally see a nude woman on the beach, or swimming in the lake. With comparisons made to the Greek goddess, Diana, her name was born. In reality, the woman's name was Alice Marble Gray, the daughter of a well to do Chicago physician. Legend tells us that she went to the dunes to soothe her broken heart, but in reality, she was going blind. So she moved into a fishing cottage and lived a simple life. In 1920 Alice met Paul Wilson. At best he was a skilled nautical man with a checkered past. They were happy together until a man was found beaten and burned on the beach. Wilson was suspected of the murders. Although the crime wasn't proven, the couple moved to Michigan City. Although Alice had two children with Wilson, he beat her and made her life miserable. After the birth of her second daughter, she either killed herself or died of uremia poisoning. Wilson disappeared but was later found in a California prison, serving time for theft. What became of Alice's daughters is a mystery. To this day, Alice returns to the dunes to ease her soul.

## Devil's Bridge
### Michigan City: County Line Rd. near LaPorte and Porter County line

The mob buried bodies here in the 1920s. Visitors capture orbs and see a transparent man who disappears.

## Gray Goose Inn
### Chesterton: 350 Indian Boundary Rd.

A little redheaded girl appears to guests. She smiles and interacts. One guest said she threw a ball to her, then disappeared. The guest was left with the ball. She put it on the table beside her bed. In the morning, it was gone. Other guests hear a child's laughter.

## Hebron High School
### Hebron: 307 S. Main St.

On a Halloween night in the 1930s, a girl waited in the gym for her date. He never showed. She got some rope from the janitor's close and hung herself in the bathroom. Today, visitors see her hanging in the bathroom during many times of the year

## Hebron Train Depot

**Hebron:** 127 S. Main St. *(the Depot is right next to the museum)*
*(aka Stagecoach Museum/Panhandle Depot)*

The majority of Hebron worked at a train station in the 1800s. A hobo haunts the depot. In October 1903, a head on train crash killed a hobo. He was buried in Hebron Cemetery. Later the Depot was known as the Whistle Stop Ice Cream Shop. A young man went to work here one day angry, as he had had an argument with his wife. He was careless and was hit by a train. Today his ghost throws pots and pans around the kitchen and turns off ovens. No business has been able to stay long. The Historical Society moved and converted the building where strange noises and footsteps are experienced.

## Historical Society of Porter County Old Jail Museum

**Porter:** 153 Franklin St.

Visitors see orbs and people have gone missing as if in a time warp. In the rope room an entity is seen and heard. A child haunts the children's room. Downstairs a woman is seen. A helmet that is part of the collection has been known to get hot where a bullet pierced a hole. Voices are heard throughout the house, especially when only one staff member is present or when staff members are separated by floors. The keys to the cell are known to move on their own.

## Housing Subdivision

**Portage:** The area is south of U.S. 20 and west of Swanson Rd.
*(Note: The area is now a new housing subdivision.)*

On site at the former Nature's Friends Nudist Colony, an excavation team unearthed Mathias Perner's cremated remains in 2005. (He was a machinist who died in 1937 and was reburied in Blake Cemetery.) A second urn was damaged at the time of excavation. The ghosts of two men are seen rising from the area where the urns were found.

## Inn at Aberdeen

**Valparaiso:** 3158 S. SR2

Items such as combs and socks go missing. The specter of a girl suspected of taking them is seen at various times and locations. In Room 305, the fireplace comes on by itself.

## Luther Cemetery

**Valparaiso:** North of US30 on Murvihill Dr.

Orbs have been captured here and voices are heard.

## Maplewood Cemetery

**Valparaiso:** South of US30 on S Sturdy Rd. and Penna Hill Dr.

Orbs have been captured here. A young woman's voice is heard saying "Maud". Orbs have been captured on film. Maud

Dau, the niece of Col. John Wheeler, who died at the Battle of Gettysburg, is buried in the cemetery. She died of TB at 15. Cemetery restorers have heard the voice and had a mischievous spirit touch them in the cemetery. One worker had her apron untied. Another worker had her bucket of ammonia tipped over.

## Old Farm House Antiques
**Hebron:** 409 S. Main St.

A woman says hello to visitors. Curtains have been pulled down.

## Old Porter County Home
**Valparaiso:** South US30 on IN2

Visitors see children playing in the home.

## Old Porter Road
**Portage:** Between Portage and Burns Harbor that line Old Porter Rd.

This area has seen its share of bad happenings. Many deaths and injuries have happened on the road and on the railroad tracks. Shadow figures are seen on the train tracks especially in the winter. Phantom dogs are also seen walking beside the road, just to disappear before your eyes. A devil dog is also spotted with yellow eyes and a semi-human form.

## Old Roller Coster Road
**Portage:** Ransom Rd
*(Note: Sycamore Rd in South Bend is also nicknamed Roller Coaster Rd. Many locals have said that Sycamore Rd is the real Old Roller Coaster Rd.)*
*(aka Ransom Road)*

Transparent and solid apparitions of automobiles chase people on this road, then disappear as quickly as they appeared. In 2002 John Blosfield was killed on this road. Some visitors say he is seen walking beside the road.

## Old Train Tracks
**Hebron:** Unknown

The tracks are the site of an alleged train crash. Its victims supposedly haunt the area

## Porter County Court House
**Valparaiso:** 16 Lincolnway

Orbs and feelings of dread are sensed in this building. The elevator moves from floor to floor without any reason. EVPs asking for help, asking if you've seen certain people have been captured.

## Porter House
**Porter:** Waverly Rd.

An old lady looks out of the front room upstairs. She is rumored to hate children. She has touched and dragged several people Shadow figures who like to play tag has been reported.

## Rasz's Gathering
**Portage:** 420 E. Commercial Ave.

Cold breezes, whispers and orbs have all been experienced at this local establishment. Televisions and lights turn on by themselves. The bar's ghosts includes the former owner Benny Lynch, who appears after closing time, and other assorted shadow figures.

## Spring House Inn
**Porter:** 303 N. Mineral Spring Rd.

A ghost boy and his mother haunt the inn. They interact with guests by smiling, approaching them, and by waving to them.

## Stagecoach Road
**Portage:** Stagecoach Rd. off US12 near Ogden Dunes

Visitors see apparitions of former residents in the area. One investigator caught a mist on film.

## Stereo Bridge
**Valparaiso:** US130 at railroad tracks south of W370N

Visitors hear the residual crash when two trains collided on the same track. You can hear the whistles blow and hear the crash and screams of agony.

## Troll's Bridge
**Valparaiso:** CR175W, south of 650N

A troll makes an appearance when you stop and talk to it.

## Valparaiso City Hall
**Valparaiso:** 166 Lincoln Way

Investigators report orbs and a feeling of being watched.

## Valpo University – Alumni Hall
**Valparaiso:** 1700 Chapel Dr.

Two children run around the hall at night. Sometimes they interact with people and talk about playing outside or playing tag. Sometimes the elevator moves from floor to floor for no reason.

## Wolf Mansion/ McCool Cemetery
**Portage:** CR700N (7 Mile Rd.) and CR450W (Wolf Rd.)
McCool Cemetery is at Central Ave. and McCool Rd.

Lights have been seen inside the mansion. In one instance a candle was lit and a shadow blew it out. A solid apparition of a man with a gun has also been reported. Visitors have captured orbs and one worker felt breathing on his neck in the basement of the building. People have been followed inside the home. The legend is that Josephus' children died of typhoid fever or small pox in the 1800s. Because of this, he hung himself in the cupola and now haunts the house.

*(Note: The story would seem to be false. Josephus McCool died of cancer on March 8, 1895 and is buried in McCool Cemetery. His wife Susan died in 1903 and is in the same cemetery. Nonetheless, it is a part of Indiana folklore.)*

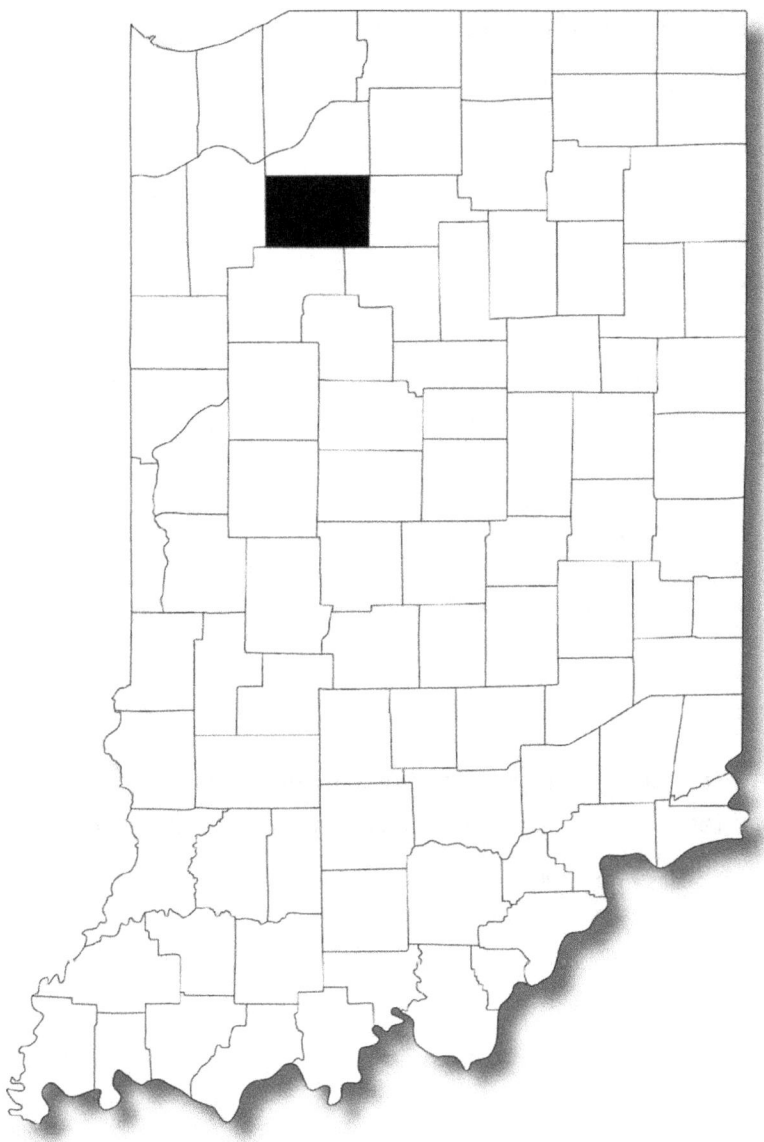

# PULASKI
# COUNTY

## City Park
**Winamac:** E.Washington St. east of S. Riverside Dr.

Two brothers were in the Civil War. One never returned home and the other lost his mind, walking along roads and creeks looking for his brother.

Investigators have captured mists by the creek. Some people have reported seeing a handsome young man walking along the creek.

## Moody Lane/Francesville Lights
**Francesville:** Division Road to Meridian Road to W150S (E Moody Rd)

The legend goes that two brothers were riding in a buggy. One brother fell out and a wheel cut his head off. The surviving brother never recovered, or gave up the search for, his sibling's head. The orange-red light that is seen is that of the other brother looking for the dead brother's head. Many times the light is seen moving row by row in corn fields.

Drive down the lane and back, and then drive down again, and park. Flash your lights three times and shut them off. The searching light is supposed to cross in front of you.

Many people claim to have experienced the legend. They also get lost without an exit and lost in a nearby cemetery (Smith Cemetery).

*(See Smith Cemetery, Francesville, Pulaski Co. and Moody Lane, Rensselaer, Jasper Co.)*

## Old St. Anne's Cemetery and New St. Anne's Cemetery
**Monterey:** West of Monterey on E700N north side of road; off of E800S on S600E.

A praying nun with a glowing halo carries a baby in this cemetery. Witnesses have seen her mouth moving as if in prayer (or possibly talking to the baby). Sometimes, visitors have heard the baby crying. Witnesses have seen the nun sitting on the roof of a barn nearby old St. Anne's.

## Smith Cemetery
**Francesville:** Corner of W100S and CR300W. Technically, this is in Jasper County

The graveyard is near Moody Lane, where a man and a woman were killed on opposite sides of the road. At midnight they cross the road to see each other. People have experienced seeing a woman dressed in tattered clothes cross the street with her arms outstretched.

# ST. JOSEPH COUNTY

## Adams Road Cemetery

**South Bend:** On Adams Rd. west of Orange Rd. just past the lake.
*(aka Adams St. Cemetery)*
*(Note: Some investigators have confused Porter Prairie Cemetery on Adams St. in Niles, MI (a short drive from South Bend, IN) for the Adams Rd. Cemetery)*

This old cemetery is said to contain unexplained mists that seem to hang over tombstones.

## Children's Campus- Indiana North Hall

**Mishawaka:** 1411 Lincoln Hwy. W.
*(aka Family Child Center)*

In 1992 North Hall was used for helping teenage girls. One nurse saw a green helium balloon near the ceiling. This type of item was forbidden, and as she was on night shift, she couldn't leave to remove it. The other staff members said to just leave it for the day shift to dispose of. The two nurses on staff did their bed checks as necessary and went about their other tasks. The balloon remained in the room with them. At 2 am, the balloon seemed to be deflating. One nurse thought that she'd dispose of it once it was finished deflating. When she looked up again, the balloon had shifted in the hallway, going through a doorway and again, popping up to the ceiling. It continued on this way until it moved back toward the nurse's station. As the nurses watched it reenter their area, it sped up and dove towards them. After it had sufficiently scared them away from the area, they watched as it went back out the way it came-under a desk, scooting along the wall of a kitchenette, and making a 90 degree turn, and then going around the room to the back of the kitchen, and dropping to the floor behind the trashcan.

One of the rooms it had stopped at was number 6, which is believed to be the room in which that a 15 year old resident died in from improper restraints in the 1980s. Odd feelings have been felt for years in this location and in the basement laundry room. In the parking lot, the staff has been bothered by knocking on cars, yet no one is around.

## Copshaholm

**South Bend:** 808 W. Washington Ave.
*(aka Oliver Mansion; aka Northern Indiana Center for History)*

Katherine Oliver haunts the Oliver Mansion. She moves items throughout the house. If you listen closely enough, you can hear her whisper to you. Also, Mrs. Standfield who was an early curator, is said to haunt the museum.

## Dreamworld

South Bend: N. Michigan St.

A woman with a dog walks the railroad tracks. Legend has it she was hit by a train and killed. EVPs of her calling for her dog have been captured.

## Hacienda Mexican Restaurant
**Mishawaka:** 706 Lincoln Way West  (100 Center)

At one time, the location used to be a mansion. The owner had an affair with a maid. She confessed to the owner's wife and who wanted nothing to do with her. The maid was sent packing. She hung herself in the attic. Now she's seen throughout the restaurant. The owner is said to have shot himself in the basement. One manager of the restaurant turned off the lights and alarm and when she would looked back, the lights would be on. She decided to take the light bulbs out of the lights. The lights still came back on; the bathroom lights would do the same thing. The water turns on as well.

## Harrison Street tracks
**Walkerton:** Harrison St.

A railroad worker was hit by a train. Today he's seen as a blood-splattered apparition. The ghost of a girl who killed herself on the track is also seen.

## Haunted House
**Lakeville:** Off U31 on 6C Road, around a curve on the left side.
*(Note: Home has been razed.)*

A lonely woman hung herself from a dining room chandelier. The house has been torn down, but a barn still remains. When the house still existed, people reported footsteps and moans. Also, there were reports of seeing a pair of bodiless feet, and sounds of the back door slamming.

## Highland Cemetery
**South Bend:** Portage Ave. and Lathrop St.
*(aka Council Oak Cemetery)*

A mysterious spectral horse is seen running through the cemetery at night. His eyes are as blue hot as a fire. He is said to have a fog precede his arrival.

## Holiday Inn City Center
**South Bend:** 213 W. Washington St.

A ghostly flight attendant visits guests in their room. The same person is seen in mirrors throughout the hotel. Legend has it that a pilot killed the flight attendant.

## Hotel
**Mishawaka:** US 933 (Lincoln Way)

This abandoned hotel is supposed to be a place to make things disappear before your eyes. Sometimes the hotel itself is said to disappear in a time warp.

## Juday Creek (Railroad) Bridge
**South Bend:** East of SR933 N and north of W. Cleveland Rd.

A train engineer who was being replaced by someone younger killed himself on the bridge. Today you can see him standing there, holding a lantern.

## Lincoln Elementary School
**South Bend:** 1425 E Calvert St

Legend has it that this was once a children's hospital. In the restrooms the faucets turn on and off randomly and the lights flicker. This seems unlikely as the school is very new.

## Mishawaka City Cemetery
**Mishawaka:** West of Main St.; South of W. Jefferson Blvd.

William Aldrich (lived at Main and Lawrence Streets), who died of TB, was buried sitting up in this cemetery. After much fanfare, and a stint on "Ripley's Believe it or Not," the casket and all of Aldrichs' possessions have disappeared. He is said to walk the cemetery and the area around his old house in search of these belongings.

## North Michigan Avenue
**South Bend:** North Michigan Ave. and Douglas Street.

A phantom, driverless car is seen speeding down the avenue, only to disappear as quickly as it was seen.

## Old Central High School
**South Bend:** 330 W. Colfax Ave.
*(aka Central High Apartments)*

The ghost of a woman and her dog haunt this area. She was run over by a train while walking the dog. At different times of the day, you can see her cross the intersection. The old school auditorium, now used as apartments, is rumored to be haunted by students.

## Old Roller Coster Road
**South Bend:** Sycamore Rd.
*(aka Sycamore Road)*

*(Note: Ransom Rd in Portage is also nicknamed Roller Coaster Rd. Many locals have said that Ransom Rd is the real Old Roller Coaster Rd)*

Transparent and solid apparitions of automobiles chase people on this road. They disappear as quickly as they appeared.

## Old St. Joseph Hospital
**Mishawaka:** 215 W. 4th St.

The Sisters of the Order of the Handmaids of Jesus Christ cared for the sick in the early days of the history of St. Joseph Community Hospital in Mishawaka. They treated the poor in economically underdeveloped areas. In the hospital as we know it today was born. It opened with 40 beds and 5 nuns as nurses. The facility was renovated in 1993 Many patients report being made comfortable or waited on by nuns in old fashioned habits. The fifth floor surgical wing is particularly active. A phantom shadow of a man is also seen. Patients report a nurse visiting them and feeling much better afterwards, only to find later no living nurse had been to see them.

## Park View Tavern
**South Bend:** 515 E Jefferson St.

Built in 1862 this structure has long been a tavern, and is reputed to have had gangland ties. The spirits are numerous in this building, including Marly, a liquor delivery driver (who later killed himself), a boy who died in the basement and several ghosts that move as shadows from room to room. Ashtrays and other items have flown off tables and crashed into walls. An apparition of a man floated above the loading dock. A male ghost was seen near the manager's office and voices have been heard in various locations. Mists and orbs have been photographed and seen and hisses have been heard on EVP recordings.

The State Theatre lounge was bought by Ken Allen. It is haunted by a 1920-ish beautiful woman with brunette hair who is clad in lavender and white. She is mostly seen in the projector room.

## Potato Creek State Park /Porter (Rea Cemetery)
**South Bend:** 25601 SR 4

Drowned children haunt the park with their cries and calls for help and for their mothers.

## Primrose Road
**New Carlisle:** Primrose Rd. off of old Cleveland Rd.

Visitors have reported an odd amount of tire damage and other car troubles on this road. No one seems to get cell phone signals on this road either. Ghosts of long gone people tell you to leave the road and not to come back. A farmhouse is said to appear from nowhere, and a woman in white will answer the door. A pond nearby has a rock in the middle nicknamed Blood Rock. It's said to move to different locations in the pond. Horses are heard running intently on the road and in the woods. A woman is said to have been killed and thrown in the pond. She's seen walking out of the pond on foggy nights.

## St. Mary's College
**South Bend:** SR933

A girl who hung herself in Le Mans Hall haunts the building. Blood spots from another girl who died appear.

## State Theater
**South Bend:** 214 S. Michigan St.

A woman haunts this location. She is described alternately as a vaudeville actress, a flapper, and a chorus girl. She appears to enjoy a change of clothing. The woman wears a white, blue, or lavender dress. She appears often when blues music is played. The theater is currently closed.

## Tippecanoe Place
**South Bend:** 620 W. Washington St.
*(aka Studebaker Mansion)*

This restaurant used to be a stately home to the Clement Studebaker family, famous for building wagons and cars. It has entertained some of the finest families including President Benjamin Harrison. It has been used as a home for deaf children and as a Red Cross Hospital. It's believed Clement Studebaker killed himself in the home. Today, the home doesn't seem to like disbelievers of the paranormal. When a waiter was asked about the ghost, he said he'd never had an experience, which caused glasses to fly off shelves.

Pictures move on the wall as if moved by unfelt wind. In one of the old nursery rooms, (now a bar on the second floor) a bottle of liquor flew off the shelf and fell to the floor at the feet of a very surprised bartender who had just declared he didn't believe in the paranormal. The security alarm consistently goes off; when the police are called, they find nothing missing, but see and hear dishes being thrown around in the basement of the building.

Other paranormal events include cold breezes, and shadow figures. Phantom restroom goers use the facilities at will.

## The University of Notre Dame
**Notre Dame:** Notre Dame has a great map on its website.

- The Potawatami lived on the original university grounds. Washington Hall on the campus is haunted by Native Americans as well as George Gipp, a former football player, who died of pneumonia after staying out past curfew and getting locked out. He has been seen in all areas but mostly resides on the stage and greenrooms. He has also pushed students, and played music. Gipp's footsteps are heard all over the building. Additionally, Washington Hall is home to a steeplejack who died during installation of lights.
- Columbus Hall is also haunted by Native Americans. Horses have been seen on the grounds outside the building and riding down the front steps.
- The Administration building is home to Father Sorin, the founder of the university. He is seen as a residual haunting.

## Uniroyal Plastics
**South Bend:** N. Hill St. was the site location.

Now razed, this company was founded in 1922 as United States Rubber Company. Building 3 was very haunted. On the fourth floor one security guard was startled by a very ordinary looking man wearing pinstriped overalls, and carrying a tool belt slung on his shoulder. The man smiled at the guard and walked out of sight into the next room. When the guard followed, he found himself alone. Despite a search, the man in overalls was not found. That same night the guard's flashlight stopped working. All security lights went out on the floors he visited, but the elevator was waiting for him. When he returned to his post and told his story, his flashlight worked again and the security lights were back on in the building.

# STARKE COUNTY

## Bass Lake (Cemetery)

**Bass Lake:** The Bass Lake Cemetery Association is at 6726 E. Kitty Ln. The cemetery is across the street.

According to legend, grass turns blood red, visitors hear evil laughter, and a werewolf roams the grounds in the evening, but there is no Bass Lake Cemetery in Starke Co. However, several spirits are seen around the lake. A man fitting the description of a pilot and a woman fitting the description of his passenger are seen at the lake (Stephanie Nottke and Bruce Groen). The smell of smoke and fuel are often sensed by investigators. The apparitions shimmer on the water and walk toward the shore.

## Craven's Factory

**North Judson:** End of Sheridan Ave. close to 502 Sheridan Ave.

James Messer killed himself in this factory. Around 1:30am, people have reported being pushed to the ground and spit on.

## Dog Face Bridge

**North Judson:** Take IN421 south to 500S turn right. Take the second dirt road on the right. There will be a sign that says bridge out and one that says road closed. Go to the bridge turn your car around facing out and get out of your car with your keys. Take US421 to 500S and turn West on 500S. Go a little ways and you will come to a stop sign. That road is 1100W. Turn North on 1100W and follow it about 1/2 mile. You will come to the bridge and a dead end.

A dog ran in front of a car carrying a couple honeymooning. The couple drove off the bridge and killed the dog in the process. The woman and dog lost their heads in the accident. The body of the woman and the head of the dog were never found.

The bridge is no longer there, but a few decaying supports mark the spot where it was. When you approach the bridge, the woman appears wearing the dog's bloody beaten head. If you don't make it back down the path to the road and past the first bridge (see directions) she will kill you.

Investigators have seen mysterious cars while investigating yet when they've listened to their evidence the sounds of the cars were not heard. Oranges and lemon verbena are smelled. Temperatures drop quickly. Electronics have lost all power, although fresh batteries and charges were verified before the investigation.

## Highland Cemetery

**North Judson:** Located on CR10 at S300W

People have reported being grabbed on the leg, and neck.

## Old Haunted Hospital
**Knox:** 102 E. Culver Rd.

This is the site of an old hotel. In the basement of the hospital, crying and screams are heard. Footsteps echo in the silent night. A janitor is still seen in the basement, mopping the floor. Patients who have passed on are still seen on the second floor.

## San Pierre Cemetery
**San Pierre:** San Pierre Rd.

In the back right side of the cemetery, in the woods, there are more stones. Visitors see figures of people walking through the woods.

# STEUBEN COUNTY

## Covenant Cemetery

**Fremont:** North of Clear Lake on Ray Clearlake Rd. (e 750 N)  and N 700 E.

In the north west part of the cemetery, a two children appear. They walk to the middle of the cemetery and disappear.

## Lakeside Cemetery

**Fremont:** South of Freemont. East of N. SR827. If you get to US80/90, you've gone too far.
GPS: 41.739182, -84.932304

Strange lights dance in this cemetery, which is surrounded by woods and bogs. Some people speculate that these are fairies or elementals that live in the woods. Others believe these are the spirits of the dead from the part of the cemetery that was relocated 25 years ago.

## McNaughton Family Cemetery

**Fremont:** NW corner of CR 700E and Ray Clear Lake Rd (CR 750N)

When you walk between the tombstones, you levitate although you are still moving forward. Cold spots and mysterious brushes with unseen people

## Old Circle Hill Cemetery/ Circle Hill Cemetery

**Angola:** Old Circle Hill Cemetery (East of Wohler St. off of W. Stocker St) Circle Hill Cemetery(Circle Hill Cemetery Rd.)
*(Note: Some people are confused as to which Circle Hill Cemetery these events have taken place.)*

The old Circle Hill Cemetery was established in 1874. Several black hooded figures have been seen in the old Circle Hill Cemetery.  The figures have been known to chase people.

## Sigma Phi Epsilon house  (at Tri State University)

**Angola:** 115 S. Darling St. (House is scheduled for demolition)

Established in 1884, Tri State University is a privately funded, higher education institution which grants baccalaureate and masters degrees. Sigma Phi Epsilon fraternity began using the house in 1968 although a new building at South Darling and S. Gale St. is currently being built. In the current building, a girl who died there several years ago haunts the home. She's been seen as an apparition, she's touched and kissed several men in the home and she's also known for taking items, but returning them in odd places later.

## Town Circle/Strand Theatre
**Angola:** 49 S Public Sq.

If you go the town circle at night and look at the Strand Movie theatre building, you will see a man with a long red beard walking around the top of the building. Some reports this man scream for a woman named "Marie" to return.

## Wing Haven Nature Preserve
**Angola:** E. of I69 on north side of W 400 N

The original part of Wing Haven was a gift from Helen Swensen received in 1983. With other sections added to the complex it now totals 264 acres and has about a mile of trails. For the last 30 years, a story has circulated about rituals being performed at the site of the nature preserve. They believe this ritual has released a being (e.g. demon, spirit, etc) into this world. The being is supposed to be contained within the stream but when you approach the stream, it will make contact with you. Visitors have experienced unexplained flat tires, electrical problems with cars, electronics, and phones. Some people have reported suicidal and other violent urges overtaking them in this section of the preserve.

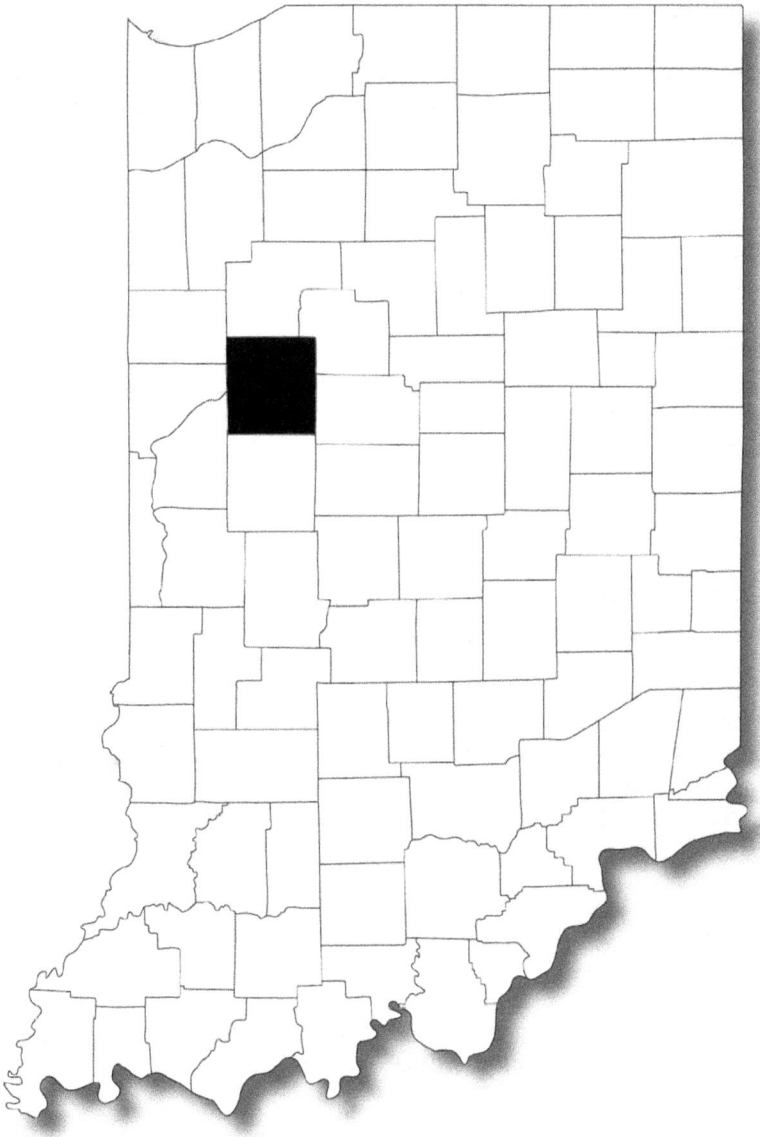

# TIPPECANOE
# COUNTY

## Baby Alice
**Lafayette:** 13th and Elizabeth Streets

In May 1857, a blue light was reported. It was nicknamed Baby Alice for a prostitute who was killed in her place of business. Today, the light is witnessed in late Fall and early Spring. Blue lights float through house and grounds. Some saw Baby Alice after her death from congestion due to poor health and consumption carrying a pitcher (or some said her heart and lungs) in her hands.

## Battle Ground Cemetery
**Battleground:** NE on Main St. (turns into Pretty Prairie Rd.)

A red eyed demon haunts this cemetery. The demon has been witnessed during the day and night walking on two hooves. With the upper body of a human, it has a face like leather. People say for each soul he takes in the cemetery, an open sore appears on his face. One scared investigator saw the demon and as he was backing away, he witnessed fewer than five open wounds on the demon's face.

## Black Rock
**Lafayette:** Near Lafayette on east of CR N 1100 E on CR E 350 N
*(Note: This is a defunct town that is now little more than woods.)*

The area, once inhabited by Native Americans, was the site for a mission and a church. Native Americans are seen here and along the river. A farmer named Fred has been seen around the area as well. He is suspected as having died of a heart attack. Another spirit named William likes attention, but has a hard time showing himself on film or EVPs. According to some investigators, William doesn't know he's dead. Other spirit is of a woman named Emma. A little boy also walks the woods in the area. Cold spots are felt and unfelt breezes make trees sway.

## Blue Bridge
**Battleground** From SR 25, turn left on 275.
*(Note: This is very close to Prophetstown.)*

A man chased by the mafia couldn't get over the bridge so he went under it. The mafia followed but mistook each other for the man and killed themselves. Today you see the residual haunting of the shooting.

## Cumberland School
**West Lafayette:** 600 Cumberland Ave.

A transparent man is seen in the window.

## Deadman's Curve

**Lafayette:** CR 450 S and CR 450 E  (7 miles SE of Lafayette)

*(aka Culver Station)*

Thirty people were killed in a train wreck  on Halloween evening 1864, when a 16 car cattle train and an 11 car passenger train (carrying hundreds of Union soldiers) collided. The speeding trains and impact, as well as cries of the injured and dying, can be heard.

## Eisenhower Bridge (Lafayette)

**Lafayette:** Eisenhower Rd. before N 400 E

A ghost of a woman with a shotgun haunts the bridge. The legend states you must flash your headlights and she will appear to talk with you.

## Harrison Cemetery

**West Lafayette:** Behind William Henry Harrison High School at 5701 North 50 West in West Lafayette.

*(aka St. Joseph Cemetery, aka Lafayette Catholic Cemetery)*

Ghosts here cry and moan in the night hours and throw rocks, sticks, and other objects. Occasionally there are sensations of being followed. Headstones move to different locations. People have been touched by icy hands.

## Historic Five Points Fire Station Museum

**Lafayette:** 1511 Main St.

Captain Nimrod Jones lives in the old No.3 fire station at Five Points. He was there when it was built in 1921, and continues to live there today as a spirit. Although no apparitions have been seen, voices have been reported as well as walking in the late evening.  A new station planned for 1710 South St. replaced the existing Five Points station which, for 79 years, has stood at the hilltop where Main, 18th, and South Streets come together.

## Greenbush Cemetery

**Lafayette:** 1408 N. 12th St.

Lights dance over the tombstones in the cemetery, especially on foggy evenings. On the far east side, a lot of paranormal activity is noted around a black stone of a man who was killed on his motorcycle. His voice has been heard and cameras have stopped working. On an erroded hill full of children's grave markers, the children are seen playing and running. People often leave gifts and trinkets for the kids.

## Lafayette Jeff High School
**Lafayette:** 1801 S. 18th St.

A former student who died in a car accident is said to walk the halls. Footsteps are heard and the person is seen along the corridor leading to the north side classrooms.

## Lahr Hotel
**Lafayette:** 117 N 5th St. at Columbia St.
*(aka The Moon Murder)*

James Moon, a Quaker farmer and blacksmith lived about 10 miles south of Lafayette. Once, he rented a room at the Lahr hotel- room 41. During his stay, a lot of banging occurred. After assuring the hotel manager that he'd pay for damages, James continued his secret work. A few days later, he left his room and met friends. The next morning, he was found dead in his room. He was killed by an ax chop from his home-made guillotine.

The hotel has now been turned into apartments, but that doesn't stop spirits from roaming the building's halls. Residents and visitors report feeling uneasy in what was the old lobby. Doors open and close on their own. Whistling and voices are heard in several apartments.

## Moses Fowler House
**Lafayette:** 909 South St.
*(aka Tippecanoe County Historical Society)*

Shadows are seen moving through the home and distinct voices are heard.

## Old City Wharf
**Lafayette:** Banks of the river between the Wabash & Erie railroad trestle (south of E. State St) and Union St.

Lafayette was a bustling hub for settlers in the early 1800s. By the 1830s, the city had a wharf along the river just a block away from the thriving downtown courthouse. As wares were transported down the river, they would be offloaded at the wharf. Not always the most savory of areas, many untold murders occurred along the banks of the river. Numerous bodies have been found floating along the waters.

In recent years, the area where the wharf stood has been redeveloped by the town. Lafayette wants ready to make "the Levee" a profitable commercial area. At night, visitors to the river bank have heard muffled conversation and have witnessed strange mists.

## Pierce Cemetery
**Lafayette:** W 600 N and N 50 W

Investigators have captured orbs and mists. A small girl in a pink and white checked pinafore skips through the darkness.

# Pythian Home

**Lafayette:** 1501 S. 18th St.

This building was erected in the 1920s for the families of the Knights of Pythias and then it was turned into an orphanage (1928) and later a nursing home (1930s). Lights turn off and on. Ghosts touch you by walking next to you or tapping you on the shoulders. Odd smells occur, such as roses and lavender. Legend has it that someone was murdered in a bathroom. After cleaning it up, they left the room and came back in just to find it as blood filled as it had been before. Another version of the story is that a woman hemorrhaged to death. Many people from the nursing home are said to have taken their lives. Safety station 13 has a door that leads to an attic, and the door opens by mysterious unseen hands. The safe in the hallway of the mansion (it weighs 600 lbs) moves on its own as well. Today, on the anniversary of the murder, the crime scene returns. Every year the Jefferson Memorial High School puts on a haunted house in the building. Screaming and banging has been heard in the elevator. Once when this happened, it got louder and louder to the point that the doors popped open, the sounds stopped and no one was in the elevator. Voices are heard; orbs captured.

# Purdue University

**West Lafayette:** Purdue Airport (Hangar 1); Earhard Residence Hall: NE corner of McArthur Dr and 1st St. Dr.

Airport (Hangar 1): Amelia Earhart haunts the hangar. Mechanics have seen a three-dimensional figure of Earhart in the hangar. Known for her lust for life and desire to know everything about aviation, Earhart is still on the job, watching mechanics work on planes and perform other tasks.

Earhart Residence Hall: Students and staff feel and see paranormal activity in Amelia's first floor corner room. They feel cold drafts, see the windows open and see a shadowy figure of Earhart in the room. They also hear the tappity-tap of an old typewriter. Snickers bars are said to appear out of thin area and sometimes Amelia Earhart appears holding one.

# Purdue University-Owen Hall

**West Lafayette:** Owen Hall on the campus of Purdue University

Wade Steffey, a freshman at Purdue University, went missing on January 13, 2007 after attending a fraternity party. For weeks, the police suspected foul play and the campus was searched except for one area, a high voltage utility closet. He was discovered by a staff member. Eventually his death was ruled an accident. Apparently he was trying to retrieve a jacket he'd lent to someone and found his way into the closet instead.

Today, students cannot go by this area without feeling a cold chill. One student claims that the body was not found in the corner, as reported, but that the utility worker opened the door and the body fell out. Students and staff alike have felt a severe feeling of depression and anxiety associated with the area. Additionally, staff members don't like going into that area because they say they've seen shadowy figures lurking about.

An interesting side note, after Wade's body was found and the funeral was over, his parents took a much needed break and went to Florida. While on a beach, his mother tracked something floating in the sky, which eventually made it into the water and onto the beach. It was a Spider-Man balloon. She believes even though he wasn't a huge Spider-Man fan, "sometimes you have to use what is available" and he sent the balloon to let them know "he knows we're there, he knows we're working on ourselves" and that eventually they would get through the painful situation.

## White Wolf
**Lafayette** North of SR 25 near Spring Vale Cemetery and Eel River.

William Lingle wrote about the haunting of his home. As early as 1872, he wrote that a blue light morphs into a white wolf appears at this location and then changes into a water beast before becoming the image of a Native American.

## William Henry Harrison High School
**West Lafayette:** 5701 N 50 W

This school is named for the man who was instrumental in killing Native Americans during the War of 1812. A teacher who died is seen in the cafeteria and in the hallways.

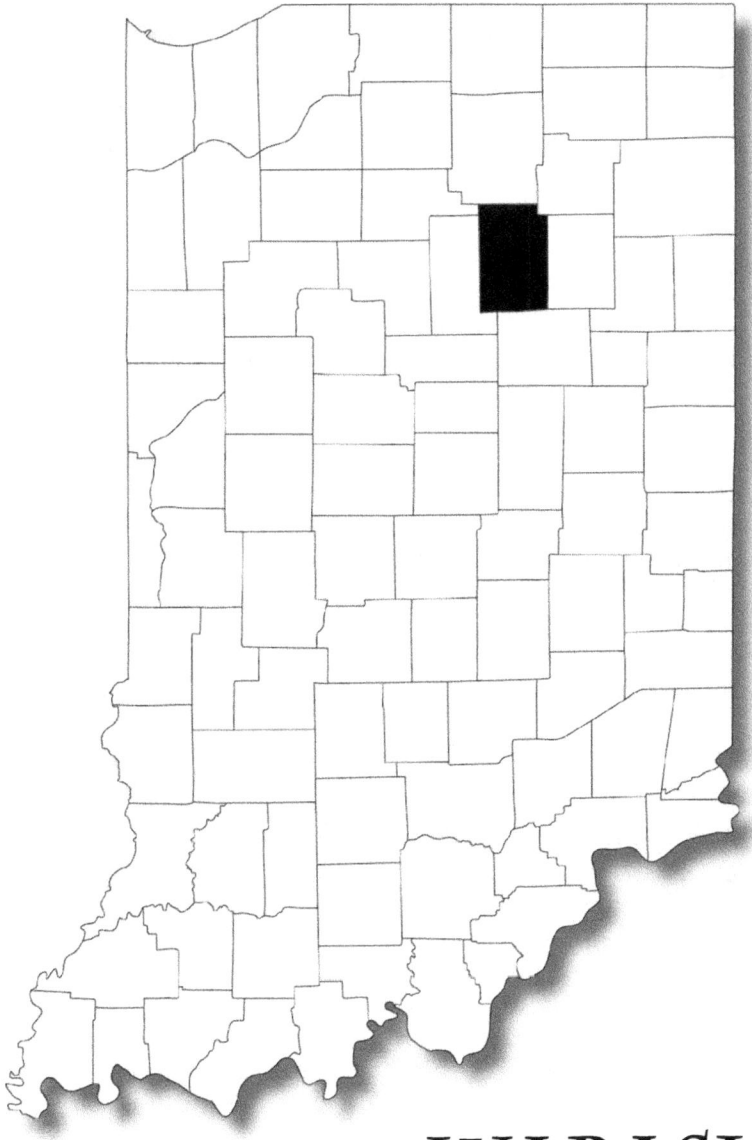

# WABASH COUNTY

## 104 East 2nd Street

**North Manchester:** 104 East 2nd Street (Brick house with apartments)

Not much is known about this location. It has two attics and hidden passages, as well as at least two known ghosts. One spirit is a tall skinny Amish-looking man in 1800s clothing. Multiple people have seen him. He does not interact but walks up stairs, and walks by visitors and residents. The second ghost is a red headed boy that walks with the man down the basement stairs.

## 207 West 4th Street

**North Manchester:** 207 W. 4th St.

Not much is known about this location, except four houses including this one caught fire and burned down. The old house had attic space without an access point. There is now a Victorian house built in its place.

Two ghosts seem to be the same or similar man at the 104 E. 2nd street location. Visitors experience feelings of a presence, feelings of dread. Doors open and close without a reason, especially if you entered a room. Pictures fall off the walls. Phantom footsteps are heard. Mother of a former tenant has been seen in a bedroom and going up stairs. Picture of same woman levitated. Doors lock without provocation. Steps are heard in living room.

## Gravel Pits

**Disko:** Travel west out of Disko on IN 114 , first right turn after E. Center St.

A woman clad in purple rags is said to roam the local gravel pits.

## Mississinewa Battle Grounds/Graveyard/Lake/Forest

**LaFontaine:** Mississinewa Lake/Forrest: 5613 E. Mississinewa Dam Road
**Battleground:** Off SR 15 north of Kem Rd.
**Graveyard:** SR 13 and Palmer Rd. (W 850 S)
*(aka Hobbitland)*

Apparitions are seen running between headstones. Blood appears on tombstones when the figures run through the cemetery. Mysterious sounds come from the woods, ranging from groans to growls and high pitched sounds. This area was closed off by the state for unknown reasons.

## Liberty Mills Public Access

**Liberty Mills:** On the south end of town is a public access site onto the Eel River. The stretch of the Eel River running by Liberty Mills is known for its canoeing and listed in several canoeing recreational guides.

Several years ago a car load of teenage girls were driving on the road. The driver lost control going around a curve, hitting several trees and ejecting the girls from the car. People said that on that night they could hear the screams of the some of the girls as they died. One even hung in a tree-a branch piercing her midsection. To this day if you go to the public access site you can hear the girls screaming and crying for help. Witnesses report hearing faint cries.

## Moonrock
**Wabash:** 3647 Old SR24 between 2 trees

Wy-nu-sa, a beautiful Native American jumped from a cliff after a duel between two men. Her favorite, was killed. Indian dancers are seen dancing around the rock.

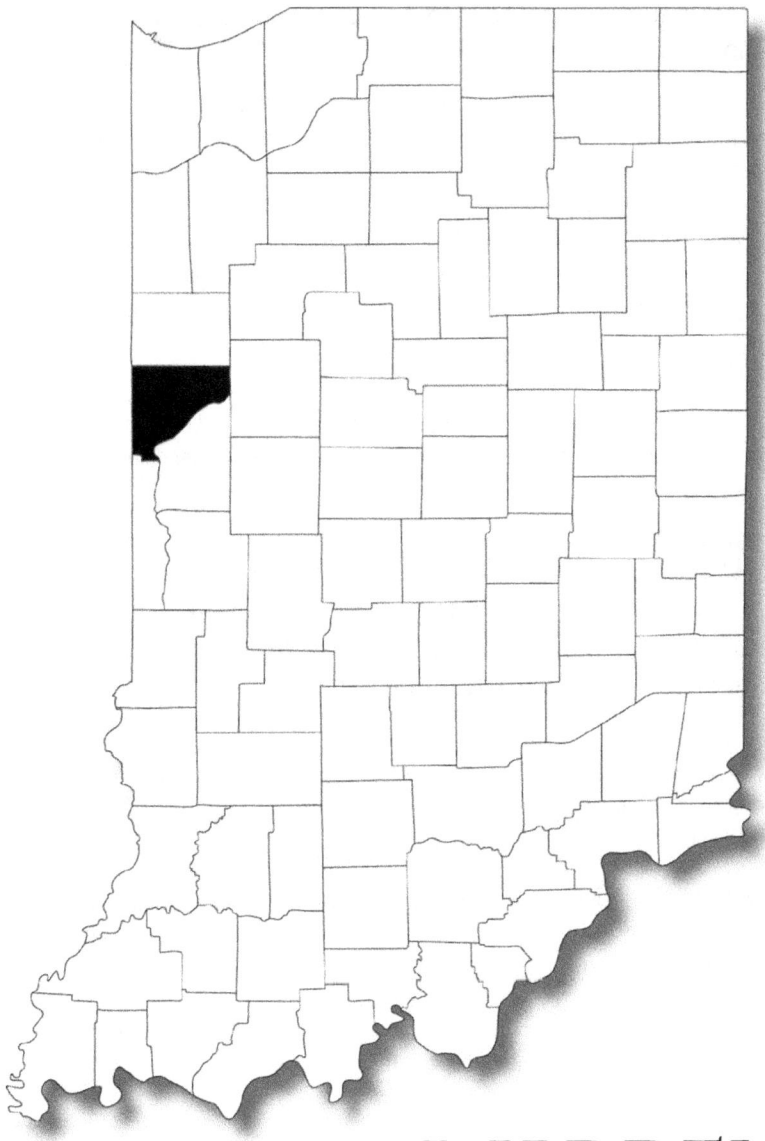

# WARREN COUNTY

## Cicott's Trading Post Park

**Independence:** East Independence Road and N800E (aka CR650N). A Trail of Death marker notes the location.

The Trail of Death went through Independence. Zachariah Cicott had a trading post on the site of the park in 1816. He was married to a Potawatomi woman and founded Independence. He is buried in the town cemetery. As someone who loved to party in life, so he does in death. He is seen walking through town, on the side of the road. He has crashed a couple of parties in the park by stealing beer and extinguishing lights. Girls report being "gently and sweetly" kissed by unseen lips- and have reported the taste of alcohol afterwards, although they do report enjoying the flavor.

## Devil's Kitchen

**Williamsport:** Center of Williamsport, under the falls.

A legendary black stove sat in the cave that runs under Williamsport. Locals believed if you went in the cave, the devil, demon or ghost would cook you in the oven. Reportedly, a child named Damon Hoffmeister died at this spot.

## Indiana Springs Company

*(aka Mudlavia Lodge; aka Mudlavia; aka Hotel Mudlavia; aka Mudlavia Spa)*

**Kramer:** Take E. Kramer Rd. (CR225E) out of Kramer. You'll come to a point in the road where E. Kramer Rd. veers left and there is a smaller road that leads right. Go to the right (E. Hunter Hill Rd.). You should see the ruins of the spa on the right.

Samuel Story discovered the springs in 1884 when he was suffering from rheumatism. Once he drank from the spa, his condition improved. Henry Kramer, for whom the town Kramer is named, developed a hotel on the site. Known as a world-class spa in the early 1900s, it burned in the 1920s. At the time, mob activity was suspected. Mobsters are supposed to be in the pond next to the former hotel.

Today harsh voices are heard. Some people have been scratched, poked and chased by unseen people running after them. Temperature drops occur. Feelings of sickness, tightness in the chest and dizziness are experienced. Orbs have been captured. The sounds of parties from mobster days are heard.

Rumors state that it burned three times, the second time killing everyone inside. People have also reported feeling someone malevolent follows them. Other visitors to the basement report a spirit who was killed in a shooting during a party.

## Locust Grove Cemetery

### Locust Grove (NE of Tab): South of CR850N on 600W

Locust Grove never got very big. In 1913 it was reported as having fewer than 100 citizens. Now a defunct town, only the Locust Grove Church and Cemetery remain. Sounds of armies walking have been heard. Some believe it is Civil War soldiers. Other people believe it is Harrison's troops moving to the Battle of Tippecanoe.

## Mound Cemetery
N600E and E700N NE of Chatterton
*(aka Round Cemetery)*

This mound-shaped cemetery is about 30 feet high. Originally a Native American burial ground, the Martindale and Little families owned the land and helped establish a "white" cemetery on site. Today, the cemetery is surrounded by a road and experiences much unrest. Native American chanting is frequently heard during the day and night, especially when it is very quiet around the area.

Legend has it that anyone who disturbs the burial site of Native Americans will have bad luck. Investigators have reported having the Native American burial site curse befall them when they've entered the site. Investigators report everything from car trouble to marital issues after they've visited the site. Additionally, misty images are often caught on photos around the upper portion of the mound.

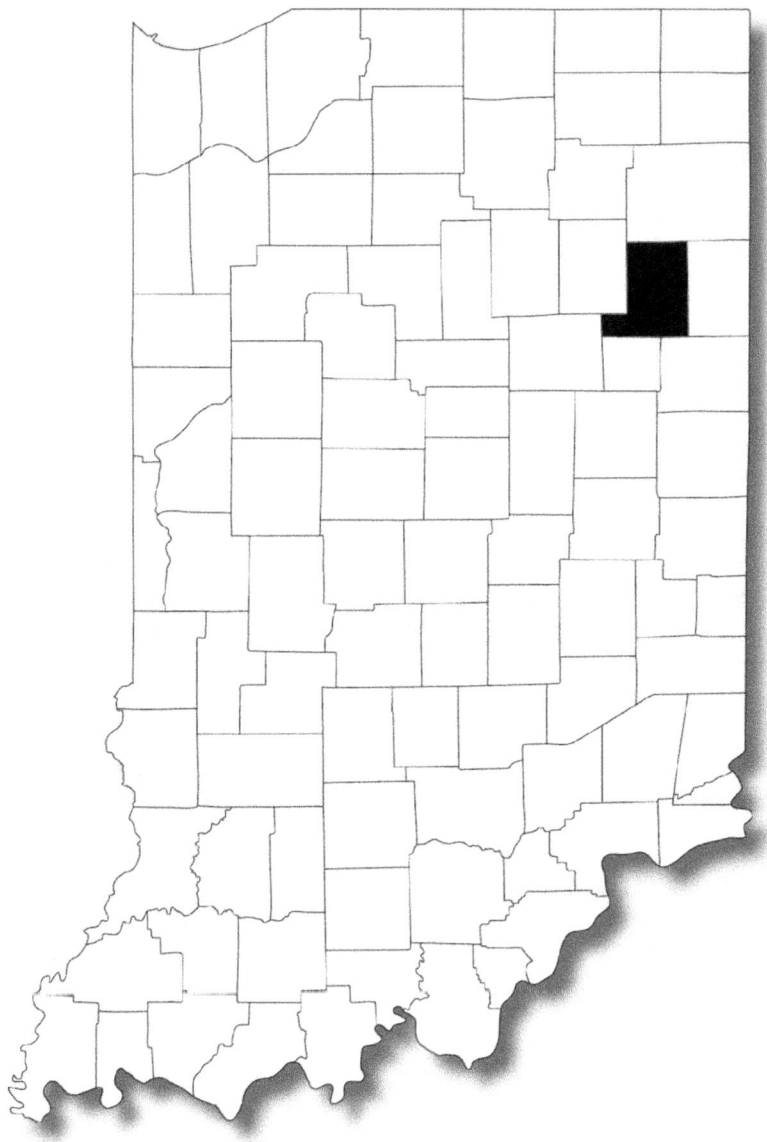

# WELLS COUNTY

## Apostolic Christian Church

**Bluffton:** East of Sunrise Way at 630 E. Dustman Rd. Locals indicate the playground was under the current parking lot

An older gentleman ran a playground for kids on the site of the Apostolic Christian Church. The children loved him, but apparently the adults didn't approve of the playground- or of him. The man was found under a red bridge in the Wabash River.

People hear children laughing and a pounding on the bottom of the bridge. An older man is seen walking in the area. Sometimes he is seen sitting on a bench that does not exist.

## Markle

*(See Huntington Co.)*

## The Rittenhouse

**Bluffton:** 218 S Main St.

Now a restaurant, the building was once home to a morgue/funeral home. Some visitors claim you can still smell the chemicals and death in the home. Mysterious occurrences include seeing spirits, presumably of the dead who passed through the building. One visitor reported walking in the upper gallery and seeing a transparent man weave his way through the guests below. He turned abruptly and smiled at her. EVP reports include disembodied voices asking for help, unintelligible murmurs and loud conversation.

## Vera Cruz (town)

**Vera Cruz:** SR 301 (S700E) and SW Center St. as well as near the bridge SW of town.

A man from the 1800s shot himself in the kitchen. He has been seen from the time of his death until present day walking into town and back out, and up the lane to the old house.

In the original home, a babysitter claimed to have seen a headless man walking up the lane to the house. The original house is no longer standing. A new home is under construction. Workers claim to have seen the same headless man, as well as the man seen in town.

## Zanesville United Methodist Church

**Zanesville:** 11811 N Wayne St

During a renovation, workers felt as if they were being watched. One worker was touched by an unseen hand. Ever since, the people are uneasy about going to the upstairs area of the oldest part of the church.

# WHITE COUNTY

## Cedarwing Park
**Brookston:** Bordered by S. Wood St., South of 8th St. E., 11th St. E. and S. Brackney St.

Misty white shapes have been reported running through the yards of neighboring homes. On calm days and nights, cold strong breezes have been experienced by paranormal investigators. Other people have reported interruptions in electronics (e.g. radios, video cameras, photo cameras).

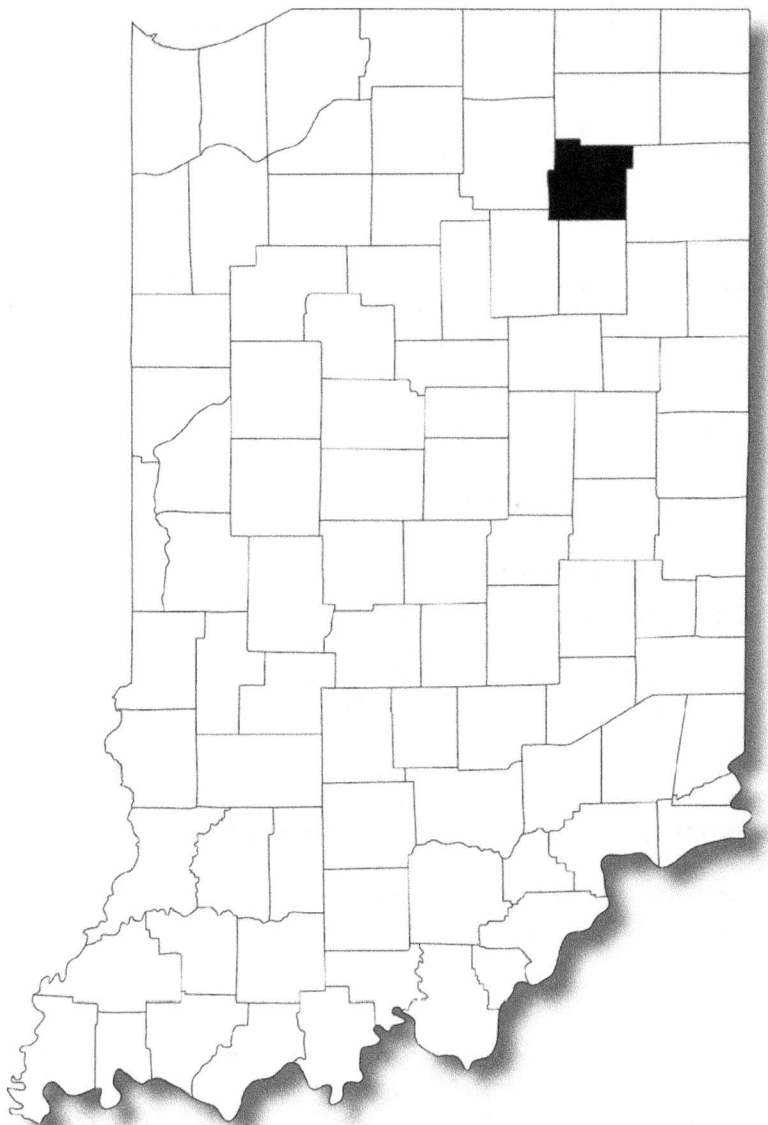

# WHITLEY
# COUNTY

## Hazelcot Castle

**Columbia City:** Marker on east side of Johnson Rd. north of De La Balme Rd. and Johnson Rd. (base only remains)

Dr. Eli Pierce and his wife Sarah moved with his family to Hazelcot in 1835. They lived a rich social life until Sarah died in 1840. In 1874 Dr. Pierce was found on the road to Ft. Wayne, dead of a heart attack. People said after his death that they saw Sarah in the library of the home. People who camped out in the home were awakened by a hand around their throat or by violent shaking.

In 1893, the home was destroyed by people scared of the paranormal. Bits of it were reused in other homes- who knows what they hold?

## Old Train Tracks

**South Whitley:** N. State St. at railroad tracks

Apparitions of girls are seen walking, and talking. One sometimes is seen holding a teddy bear.

## Old Whitley County Sheriff's Home and Jail

**Columbia City:** Corner of Market and Post & Mail Streets

This old jail and home was built in 1875 and designed by J.C. Johnson, who designed many Indiana Courthouses and jails. The beautiful stone masonry was completed by William Carr. On the 10 most endangered landmarks list, this building is home to spirit activity.

History shows Charles Butler murdered his wife Abigail and is said to haunt this old jail, which is no longer used for incarceration. It is sometimes used as a haunted house during Halloween, yet real paranormal activity occurs as well.

Employees and visitors have experienced hearing footsteps and scraping on wall. The building also has one door that will not stay closed no matter how many times it is shut. On the third floor, a woman's footprints appear on the wall as if painted in ash. If you mention Abigail's name on the third floor, unexplained activity, such as lights turning off or on and items moving, occurs.

Shadow figures are seen peering out from windows. Lights are seen in windows at night. A woman had a conversation with an older man who was standing outside the building, taking care of the lawn. He talked to her about the history of the place. She turned to look at the building for a second and when she turned back to him, he was gone.

## Parkview Health

**Columbia City:** 353 North Oak Street

Part of this facility was an old funeral home. The electrical system seems to short out at odd times. Chairs and other equipment move by unseen hands. The activity increases in the evening and during the Fall. Various people, including children, have seen people that others could not see.

## Whitko High School
**South Whitley:** End of W. Wayne Street at Big Blue Ave.

Legend has it one student dies every year. An old woman forewarns people of this each year when school starts.

# Index

## Z